STORYquest
the Writer, the Hero, the Journey

by

Laura Lentz

Published by LITerati academy
Kilauea, Hawai'i 96754
https://LITerati.academy

Cover & Illustration by Philip Brautigam
Book Interior Designed by Philip Brautigam

Typography
Titles: Paralucent
Headlines: Playfair Display
Body: Expo Serif Pro

First Edition — First Printing

Copyright ©2020 by Laura Lentz

All rights reserved.

No part of this publication may be reproduced in any form whatsoever without written permission from the author, except for brief quotations embodied in literary articles or reviews.

LITerati academy
ISBN 978-0-578-23668-1

For my students

Contents

Prologue / vii

How to use the STORYquest STORYlabs / ix

Grief and the Hero's Journey / xvii

1 The World of Before / 1

2 The Call to Growth / 19

3 Refusal of the Call / 33

4 Mentors & Angels / 47

5 Jumping into the Portal / 67

6 Put to the Test / 83

7 Rock Bottom / 99

8 Celebrations / 117

9 Trouble Again / 131

10 Rebirth / 147

11 Bringing the Magic Home / 161

12 Integration / 175

STORYquest Resources / 189

Gratitude / 193

Index — Poetry & Inspiration / 195

"We must break to become anything different than what we are. Whether it's a broken bone, a broken habit, a broken marriage or a broken heart, something must be destroyed before something new can be created.

It's the hardest, most soul-wrenching experience — breaking to the utmost of what you always thought you were — but beautifully brazen and raw, wild as a black stallion and so worth the ride."

Kristie Stout from The Secret Lives of Women

Prologue

I met a man a few weeks after my father died. He was unlike any man I had met before. This guy had edge and I went to him, dripping in lust. And I felt like he was my moon. Over time, I found him to be critical, just like my father. And he laughed with his whole body, just like my father. And he played musical instruments, just like my father.

And he wanted to keep me small, just like my father.

One morning when I was writing, the man I was dating came out for a glass of water and said, "Why do you think anyone is interested in your stories?"

And this also reminded me of my father, who tore my pen pal letters to my cousin in half and threw them in the trash because I wrote too much about myself. He insisted I not use the pronoun "I", which is nearly impossible for an eleven-year-old, It was painful to have my father repeatedly tear my pages out from underneath me and throw them away. I felt as if he was throwing a part of my identity into the trash.

Though my mother was the writer, journalist and author, my father's scrutiny became a blessing. Through this exercise, he taught me how to see, and in teaching me how to see the world around me, my father taught me how to write. What felt like abuse turned out to be a gift.

My first letter to my cousin was about the crab apple tree outside our kitchen window that finally bloomed after our family cat was buried under it. I wrote about the neighbor's Irish Setter that gave birth next door, and how blind puppies find the nipple by scent.

My father taught me to look at the world around me and to find the details and magic there.

Recently, a poet emailed me to say her mother asked her to stop sending her poems she had written. I knew this woman's father had loved her words, and it felt like a family dynamic more than a critique on her writing ability. But she quit my class, even though she just returned to writing after a long hiatus. And I had to take a deep breath, because this writer's work was so astonishing.

And the same day she wrote to me, a friend called me and said he didn't understand why so many writers follow my stories on social media.

And I understood what these people all have in common – they need to see us small, because they are afraid of their own big, their own unmet potential.

This is why I'm writing to you, we are living in times that demand us to no longer stay silent, times that are asking us to grow. Don't let anybody keep you small. Don't live in the wake of someone else's fear. It's okay to take up space, to stand in your Big — and it's okay to shed boyfriends or friendships or professional relationships that are keeping you small. If your family is not supportive, stop telling them about your dreams, and instead, share your stories with people who can receive them with grace.

This workbook is an invitation for you to write your story.

Because your stories matter:

> To me,
>
> to the world
>
> and to you.

Write them. Publish them. Shout them from stage with pages in your hand, with tears streaming on them and ink running into your fingers.

If one person loves it or a hundred thousand love it, it doesn't matter. You threw a life raft into an audience and someone is floating on your words.

I will be here for you — and this workbook will be here — to remind you to embrace your BIG and your whole journey.

Don't let anyone keep you small. No matter how much they proclaim to love you.

Because love is not small.

How to Use the STORYquest STORYlabs

When you begin to think about writing your story, the not-yet Hero may be an ordinary person, the You of Before. If you love her, she will love you back and grow before your eyes. You can sing to her and whisper in her ear. When you begin writing her, she will be challenged and perhaps follow you like a shadow. Soon, she will leave your shadow to step into her own destiny, which also may have also been your destiny. You are her, and she is you. And no one — not even you, can ever truly tear you two apart. This is how the past, present and future will shape your story.

The Shape of a Story

The Hero's Quest is as old as cave drawings and as new as your story waiting to find its way to the page. Joseph Campbell, in his groundbreaking book "A Hero with a Thousand Faces" reminds us of the patterns and rhythms of storytelling. While it's true storytelling has a shape that can be traced back to the early days of the recorded world, every story is unique, and despite patterns that show up in most stories, no two stories are the same — not every pattern shows up the same way in every story.

When creating, we must be careful not to fall into the universal archetype, or try too hard to fit our story into a formula. The purpose of this workbook is to act as a framework to support your exploration. The details that will emerge from this experience will be unique to your creative process and unique to you.

Storytelling is Sacred – Simplify the Process

After teaching writing classes for many years, I know that storytelling is a sacred exploration. It's what we have to pass onto to each other for knowledge, history, cultural reference and connection. So many writers have asked me the best way to write their books, which is why I put this workbook together. The content has been taken from my ongoing class where I dissected the Hero's Journey for book writers, through examples from popular memoirs and poetry books that tell whole stories.

Some of the information I discovered about the Hero's Journey felt complex and difficult to put into practice — and it was geared to the film industry. I simplified the journey, offering literary examples, because written stories often unfold differently than cinema. The literary examples I have chosen prove every book has elements of the Hero's Quest — and yet each book is incredibly unique in the way it illustrates the stages.

Literary Inspiration Raises the Creative Bar

This book offers inspiration in the form of quotes, poetry and segments from literature. It's essential to be inspired before we write, because every writer is writing on the backs of every other writer. Someone else's story will inspire your story. We are all interconnected inside the giant web of the creative process, through almost invisible threads. It's why my writing groups are so popular — because creativity is contagious. When you experience another writer's journey through story, you are reminded of a deeper part of yourself. And when you write your story, someone else's soul is ignited to write their story. This is how storytelling never ends, how all of our journeys are so deeply connected.

Art informs the creation of new art. This is why I recommend writing immediately following the inspirational segments of the book. I offer writing warm-ups in the form of short, two minute exercises based on each stage of the journey — STORYlabs — opening writing prompts to help you create content for every stage of the Hero's Quest. While the prompts address writers creating memoir, they can be used for fiction.

All the prompts are segmented by the Stages of the Hero's Quest, and do not have to be done in order.

Find Your Truths Against the Clock

Timed writing exercises are essential to get to any truth faster. If we write without over thinking or over processing, we will let The Universe do its magic with us. I have been teaching students for over ten years and I know writers who quit their day jobs to write books. When they have too much time on their hands, their writing often stalls out. It's not necessary to quit your day job - all that time on your hands results in too much pressure. You can write an entire book in thirteen-minute segments. I have witnessed this many times.

Editing a book is hard work and takes longer — but creating the book should be fun and organic and can be written inside an active creative community. This book shows you the way.

Every stage of a Hero's Quest does not show up in every successful story or book, because every stage is not necessary for you to have a compelling story. Exploring all the stages will ensure you have overturned all the essential creative elements.

A Hero's Quest is About Straddling Life and Death

Inside the Quest, every main character faces life and death at every turn. The Hero may not brush against actual death, but an awareness of their mortality will inform them how to live. As Frank Ostaseski has written in his book, *The Five Invitations*, "Life and death are a package deal. You cannot pull them apart."

Maybe Your Manuscript Needs Help

If you have a manuscript, you can workshop your manuscript through the prompts inside this workbook. You can utilize the exercises to see what additional stories may come out of you to include in your book, or it may show you the details that might be missing.

Practice, Practice, Practice

Lastly, if you have never thought of writing a whole book, this workbook will help you practice the art and craft of writing your stories. The practice of writing – putting words on a page — is key to becoming an artful storyteller. Inspiration and a powerful framework are key to practice. This workbook welcomes you to your practice with exceptional literary inspiration and a simple structure to help you craft something that might surprise you, by turning your words into a bigger story!

After I became an editor, reading for enjoyment felt more challenging. However, I still read hundreds of pages a day for enjoyment, trying to silence my inner editor. I carefully selected five memoirs to use in this course. All of the books I chose are very different. Even though every book is a memoir, all the exercises in this course are equally effective for fiction.

Syncreation

Years ago I made up a word — *Syncreation* — to describe what I witness every day in my writing groups. When writers create in groups, writing silently together, something magical enters the creative space. There's energy and synchronicity that that can't be explained by science.

When I first began teaching writing, I was often astonished when writers who were creating silently together read back their work and three of ten writers had red bicycles in their stories, or the same small town in Texas. Or four writers mentioned the Golden Gate Bridge. Over the years I have come to understand that writing is a communal act, and we are all creating with and through each other. We are not creating alone. Instead, we are informed by all the writers that came before us, and the energy of the writers creating with us. In so many ways we are creating side by side, always inside each other's creative process.

Gender & The Hero's Quest

You will find me alternating STORYlabs between the pronouns *he, she* and *they* when addressing the Hero. The Hero's Quest belongs to everyone.

Recommended Books:

Excerpts from the following books are used throughout this workbook to illustrate examples of the Hero's Quest.

You Are Not Alone
A Heartfelt Guide for Grief, Healing and Hope

Debbie Augenthaler

You Are Not Alone takes readers into Debbie's personal journey of grief, beginning with the first gripping chapter, when her husband dies unexpectedly in her arms. Throughout the book, Debbie takes readers by the hand and offers them gentle insights and suggestions for healing and hope, while sharing her powerful story of loss and the spiritual journey that led her to know love never dies. Debbie's book is a reminder that losing someone we love can catapult us into a Hero's Journey, if we are willing to accept our fate and step into the journey.

The Color of Water,
A Black Man's Tribute to His White Mother

James McBride

In *The Color of Water, a Black Man's Tribute to His White Mother*, journalist James McBride retraces his mother's footsteps and, through her searing and spirited voice, recreates her remarkable story. This book takes us into two Quests —the author's and his mother's, as he retraces her life to discover the Jewish heritage and the world she left behind. Over two years on the New York Times bestseller list.

the Writer, the Hero, the Journey

Stag's Leap
Sharon Olds

Stag's Leap is a heart opening and heart-breaking sequence of poems where Sharon takes us through her divorce after thirty years of marriage to a man she loves. This refreshing and spellbinding collection of confessional poems weaves a Hero's Quest through Sharon's recall of the heart, reminding us how the self, diminished by loss, survives the journey - not only in life, but also through art. *Stag's Leap* sold out in 2013 after winning the Pulitzer Prize.

The Beggar King and the Secret of Happiness
A True Story
Joel ben Izzy

The Beggar King and the Secret of Happiness is that rare, magical book—a book that tells a beautiful story but also shows us how the tales we learned when we were children shed light on our adult lives. Steeped in mythology and wonder, Joel ben Izzy's Hero's Journey begins on the day the magical storyteller lost his ability to speak. We go on this journey with him, turning the pages to discover the secret of happiness.

The Chronology of Water
Lidia Yuknavitch

In *The Chronology of Water*, Lidia Yuknavitch broke a "memoir mold" - showing us how to weave back and forth in time expertly, how to drop us into the chaos of her Hero's Journey without shame. We rise with her and fall with her, each and every time, deep into her personal story of chaos, loss, sexuality, gender, violence and the complexity of family. Publisher's Weekly says "this powerful memoir bursts open with the birth of her stillborn daughter and from there the events of her life swim in and out between each other, without chronology. Yuknavitch repeatedly returns to the image of life's fragments being swept along, as if by a current."

STORYquest

I envy the tree, how it reaches but never holds.
Mark Nepo

Ithaka

C. P. Cavafy Translated by Edmund Keeley

As you set out for Ithaka
hope your road is a long one,
full of adventure, full of discovery.
Laestrygonians, Cyclops,
angry Poseidon—don't be afraid of them:
you'll never find things like that on your way
as long as you keep your thoughts raised high,
as long as a rare excitement
stirs your spirit and your body.
Laestrygonians, Cyclops,
wild Poseidon—you won't encounter them
unless you bring them along inside your soul,
unless your soul sets them up in front of you.

Hope your road is a long one.
May there be many summer mornings when,
with what pleasure, what joy,
you enter harbors you're seeing for the first time;
may you stop at Phoenician trading stations
to buy fine things,
mother of pearl and coral, amber and ebony,
sensual perfume of every kind—
as many sensual perfumes as you can;
and may you visit many Egyptian cities
to learn and go on learning from their scholars.

Keep Ithaka always in your mind.
Arriving there is what you're destined for.
But don't hurry the journey at all.
Better if it lasts for years,
so you're old by the time you reach the island,
wealthy with all you've gained on the way,
not expecting Ithaka to make you rich.

Ithaka gave you the marvellous journey.
Without her you wouldn't have set out.
She has nothing left to give you now.

And if you find her poor, Ithaka won't have fooled you.
Wise as you will have become, so full of experience,
you'll have understood by then what these Ithakas mean.

Republished with permission of Princeton University Press, from Selected Poems by C. P. Cavafy ©1972; permission conveyed through Copyright Clearance Center, Inc.

*In everything we do, as we are shaped by
life events and inevitable traumas, something is left
behind or lost to us.*

Debbie Augenthaler

Grief & The Hero's Journey
Debbie Augenthaler

The power of grief has informed art since the beginning of time. When a trauma happens, it unleashes this power, which can be constructive or destructive (and often both). If we don't harness grief's power, it can lead to terrible events. The Greeks understood this, writing about the depth of pain in grief and the power of human emotions in Greek tragedies like Antigone, Oedipus Rex, and the Odyssey, classics that endure and captivate us to this day, some 2,500 years later.

The Greek word for wound is trauma. And aren't wounds of the heart the very essence of what makes a powerful Hero's Journey? Every Hero's Journey has an element of grief in its archetypal story pattern, because grief is the natural response to the loss of something or someone. In everything we do, as we are shaped by life events and inevitable traumas, something is left behind or lost to us.

Learning to harness the power turns the details of our grief experiences into compelling stories. Writing about grief helps to heal not only the writer, but also the reader. Grief is a universal experience and it helps those who are grieving to hear other people's stories and how they coped and survived.

Bryan Doerries, a writer and theater director said,

> *"Through tragedy, the great Athenian poets were not articulating a pessimistic or fatalistic view of human experience; nor were they bent on filling audiences with despair. Instead, they were giving voice to timeless human experiences—of suffering and grief—that, when viewed by a large audience that had shared those experiences, fostered compassion, understanding and a deeply felt interconnection. Through tragedy, the Greeks faced the darkness of human existence as a community."*

And this is what writing about our own Hero's Journey can do. We can face the darkness together and light sparks of hope at a time when there may be none. The deeply felt interconnection of suffering and transcendence weaves us together in a shared human experience.

The strewn and tangled wreckage that litters our lives is the precious raw material from which great beginnings are forged.

Craig D. Lounsbrough

STORYlab1

the WORLD of BEFORE

Ordinary doesn't mean normal

 **STORY**lab1

"The World that awaits you may end up just as good as The World of Before or better, and if you had to let go of someone you love, bearing the grief will alter you in ways you can't possibly understand.

You just have to let go of the old world you inhabited, and realize The Universe has already written the first chapter of your Hero's Quest. All you have to do is open the book of your intuition, feel your wings and fly."

Laura Lentz

the **WORLD** of **BEFORE**

The World of Before
The Foundation of Your Story

If the reader does not know where you came from, they cannot understand your journey. The adventure does not begin here, but the story does. This is a foundational time to share with your reader. In the introduction I mentioned time and memory. In many books, The *World of Before* can show up later in the book, or it can show up throughout the book in a series of flashbacks. In *The Glass Castle*, Jeanette Walls starts in the present before going back. This the foundational time before everything changes.

This part of a story is important, because it shows one thing AGAINST another thing. The present and the future in contrast with the past. Every story needs contrast. The next stage is The *Call to Growth*. If we don't know where you came from, we may not understand where you are headed or why.

Most Journeys of Place
Lead to the Inward Journey

I don't know a Hero's Quest that doesn't also include an Inward Journey. This is a journey that may not involve travel, may not involve physically changing your address. This is a journey of the mind, the heart and the spirit. In every good story the Hero grows and changes, making a journey from one way of being to the next. The journey may be from love to hate and back to love, or it may take the reader from despair to hope. The Hero may be physically or emotionally weak and become strong. The emotional component of a Hero's Quest is what makes it relatable, it's what hooks the reader and makes a book a page-turner, a story worth reading to the end.

STORYlab1

When You are in The World of Before
the following scenarios may apply to your story:

1. **You are in a world that doesn't resonate for you, and you may be trying to make it work or the Hero may have become complacent.** The Hero in *The World of Before* may be marking time, living unconsciously day to day, or stuck in a routine that has made them slightly restless. In this scenario, they may have no wound that is obvious to the reader. Perhaps they are a doctor caring for patients and feeling like they are not out of place in the environment, as if they doesn't belong anymore. Perhaps they are not in accord with the culture or environment that surrounds them. In this case, the Hero may be in denial and telling themselves everything is alright. A husband may say, "my wife is nice, she's a good mother" — and be overlooking other issues. A doctor may say, "my patients need me." Sooner or later a force will enter the lives of this Hero, and it will no longer be possible for them to mark time.

2. **The Hero is hiding their magic, or has not recognized their hidden magical powers.** In this scenario, the Hero may feel wings tickling on shoulder blades. They may have a special skillset they are suppressing, or they may not have discovered their magical powers yet. Maybe they had a psychic dream and may be avoiding the message. They may begin to realize their magical powers and hide them in *The World of Before*, knowing nobody would understand.

3. **You are leading a happy life before a Big Wounding Event.**

   In Joel Ben Izzy's story *The Beggar King and the Secret of Happiness*, we understand his *World of Before* without having to see all the details, because his wounding event is so dramatic. We know he is in a happy marriage and he has children he loves. We also know his voice has been taken away, and we see him — a professional storyteller, father and husband — strangely moving through life without a voice.

   In Debbie Augenthaler's book, *You are Not Alone*, she opens with her wounding event - her husband dying in her arms - but throughout the book we get glimpses of *The World of Before* as her grief unfolds. Both books are wonderful examples of a Hero's Journey triggered by a wounding event.

the **WORLD** of **BEFORE**

SUMMARY: The World of Before

- It's the place where you came from last.

- It's the place where you were before your journey began.

- It's the context.

- It's Home Base.

- It's as Different as possible from where you are going.

- May seem boring and calm, but seeds of excitement and challenge are emerging within that world.

- We are glimpsing the Hero's problems and conflicts motivating them to change.

STORYlab1

Sometimes it is necessary to reteach a thing its loveliness.
Galway Kinnell

the WORLD of BEFORE

LITERARY examples

An Ordinary Boy
C. Dale Young

A fascicle of feathers in my hand, hand
frantic and shaking, my arm holding my hand
as far away from my body as possible—I am disgusted.
I cannot pull out the central stalks of my wings
where they protrude from between my shoulder blades,

but I can strip every tuft of feathers from them
to bare those cartilaginous stems as they rise
from my back, stalks stripped perfectly
clean so as to better tuck them along my spine,
hide them, make them invisible beneath my clothing.

I was so foolish then, a teenager not yet able
to accept what he was. When my wings blackened,
withered, and fell off, I was beyond happy.
They would stay dormant sometimes as long as
three months. Sadly, they always came back.

In the bathroom mirror, I can see myself offering
a cluster of feathers to myself, as if to say:
Take this from me and I will be forever grateful.
But the me that is a trick of light on glass
is uncaring, offers them back immediately.

If I concentrate, if I think hard on it, I can move
my wings, and I practice in the bathroom mirror.
But these wings cannot support my weight,
cannot buoy me on even a strong gust of wind.
What good are wings if you cannot fly?

What good is this ridiculous secret I am asked
to keep? With the feathers ripped cleanly away,
I tuck the stems along my spine. I bandage them down—
cloth wound under my armpits, tightly wound
around my chest. I fashion myself into an ordinary boy.

An Ordinary Boy from **The Halo** *©2016 by C. Dale Young.
Reprinted with permission of Four Way Books. All rights reserved.*

the WORLD of BEFORE

Fertile Ground
Wendi Romero

Every once in awhile
I withdraw from my familiar.
I lie on my back and watch
clouds go by, or head out
for a long quiet drive,
not all things are able
to grow in one spot,
so sometimes I set my sight
on somewhere else.
It often takes bravery
and the risk of my utter
aloneness to seek out
that unknown patch of
fertile ground where only
I was meant to blossom.

*Fertile Ground from **Reflections of the Heart** ©2018 by Wendi Romero. Reprinted with permission of Wendi Romero.*

STORYlab1

READ

Many authors show the Hero unable to perform a simple task in the ordinary world. By the end of the story, she has learned, changed, and can accomplish the task with ease.

The ordinary world also provides backstory embedded in the action. The reader must work a little to figure it all out, like getting fed the appetizers, a little at a time. This engages the reader.

The Chronology of Water

Lidia Yuknavitch

Chapter Three

The Color of Water

James McBride

Chapter One

Stag's Leap

Sharon Olds

Love Page 31

the
**WORLD
of
BEFORE**

create**YOUR**story

STORYlab1

Writing Warm-Ups

Two-minute warm-ups prepare you for the longer writing exercises.

Set a timer for one-minute.

Use the first sentence as a starter sentence, then write for another minute using the second sentence.

Repeat.

WRITING WARM-UP 1

Once upon a time.
[write for one minute]

And every day after that.
[write for another minute]

WRITING WARM-UP 2

I would have known them anywhere.
[write for one minute]

Is that where I begin?
[write for another minute]

the WORLD of BEFORE

Pre-Writing Exploration
We Are Always Who We Are

Who we become is always in us. Who our characters become is inside of them all along.

In every story, there is the idea that the true nature inside someone has been muted or silenced. Or it is a small seed developing, not given enough water to grow.

Choose the character or who you were in the beginning of your story, before any call or transformation occurs.

Pre-Writing Instructions:

Write your name or character name at the top of the page. Complete each exercise writing for two minutes on each.

List Suppressed Magical Qualities

*Write about the real you hidden inside of you.
Make a list of your magical qualities that you suppressed.*
[write for two minutes]

List the Ways You Hid

*Make a list of all the ways you hid the real you
from the people around you.*
[write for two more minutes]

STORYlab1

Create Your Story
Writing Instructions:

Choose the writing prompt that inspires you. Later, you can explore each prompt.

Write for thirteen minutes without stopping, or overthinking your content. Set your timer!

1 DEFERRING YOUR DREAMS

Write about the you that was deferring your dreams, and the price you paid for your deferred dreams.
[write for 13 minutes]

2 A TYPICAL DAY

Write about a typical day in your Before World.
[write for 6.5 minutes]

*Then, switch and write your imaginary fantasy day
— how you really wanted your world to be.*
[write for 6.5 more minutes]

3 HIDING YOUR MAGIC

*— Write from your Writing Warmup 1 —
Write how you had to hide your real self and your magical qualities
in your ordinary world, or write about a time
your magical qualities were exposed.*
[write for 13 minutes]

4 NOT FITTING IN

Write a story of not fitting in.
[write for 13 minutes]

the **WORLD** *of* **BEFORE**

Create Your Hero

A Hero is the character in the story that goes through the most transformation.

Every Hero has major flaws — this is what makes the Hero relatable to the audience, and why we root for the Hero and believe in them.

These exercises are designed to show character traits of the Hero before their journey.

Writing Instructions:

Complete each of these three exercises, writing for two minutes on each. Set your timer!

1 LIST YOUR HERO'S FLAWS

Make a list of character flaws that could stop the Hero from getting what they want. Or describe the ways in which the Hero is their own worst enemy. How your young Hero is a victim of their own personality flaws.
[write for 2 minutes]

2 THE BIGGEST FLAW

Circle the biggest flaw from your list of your Hero's flaws. Write to the single flaw that could lead to the downfall of the character and why this flaw will take him down.
[write for 2 minutes]

3 LIFE-SAVING FLAW

Write to the single flaw that could end up saving their life.
[write for 2 minutes]

STORYlab1

Create Your Story

Writing Instructions:

Choose the writing prompt that inspires you. Later, you can explore each prompt.

Write for thirteen minutes without stopping, or overthinking your content. Set your timer!

1 BEGINNING SEED

Write about the seed that began the Hero's World of Before and how that seed started to grow.
[write for 13 minutes]

2 SEEING THE BEGINNING

Write about the beginning, wherever your beginning was… when you began to see the world through a different lens.
[write for 13 minutes]

3 THE FLAWED HERO

Write about looking back with compassion on your young Hero self — the former you. Incorporate at least one flaw.
[write for 13 minutes]

Not everything that is faced can be changed, but nothing can be changed until it is faced.

James Baldwin

STORYlab2

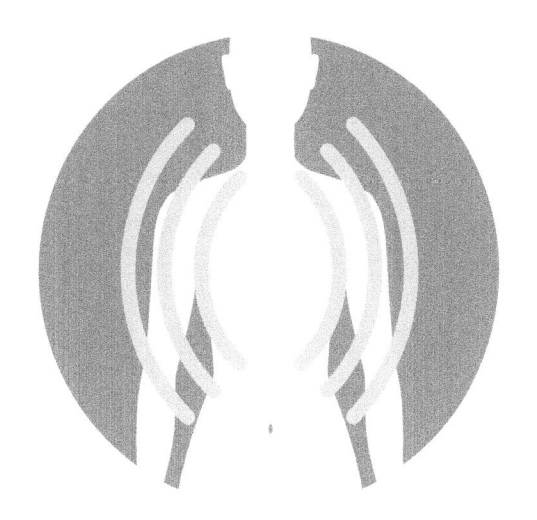

the CALL to GROWTH

The inner voice, a time for change

"To die will be an awfully big adventure."
J.M. Barrie – Peter Pan

"Nobody who says, 'I told you so' has ever been, or will ever be, a Hero."
Ursula K. Le Guin

"If you are always trying to be normal, you will never know how amazing you can be."
Maya Angelou

*"To venture causes anxiety, but not to venture is to lose one's self....
And to venture in the highest is precisely to be conscious of one's self."*
Søren Kierkegaard

"No, no! The adventures first, explanations take such a dreadful time."
*Lewis Carroll
— Alice's Adventures in Wonderland & Through the Looking-Glass*

"I feel the need to endanger myself every so often."
Tim Daly

The Call to Growth
Where the seed inside of you begins to germinate!

This stage of storytelling is necessary to get a good story rolling. We are going along in life and then suddenly we have a moment that begins to shape our dreams – a door cracks open and we can see another world – the adventure is calling to us, and we venture into the forest, into the idea of visiting a foreign country, into the arms of another person. Perhaps you have always wanted to see Vietnam and everywhere you go you overhear people talking about Vietnam, or when you flip the channels on television there is a documentary about people who not only visited the country, but moved there.

At first the *Call to Growth* will be a whisper, a noticing, a knock on your door. You may receive an invitation that will lead you to a wedding where you will meet someone who will invite you to do something, go somewhere, or step into another version of yourself you have forgotten.

The *Call to Growth* may be a billboard you pass every day, and on this day you read it and it was just the message you needed – it's any triggering incident. It's a form of initiation – it's a catalyst to taking a personal or professional leap. There is rarely ONE *Call to Growth* – but in this part of your story, this will be the FIRST *Call to Growth*. As you are on your journey you may receive many calls, and they will show up again and again, but in this part of the framework of your story, it's the initiating *Call to Growth*.

In this stage of the story, the Hero knows it's time for a change, or perhaps change is long overdue. Or perhaps, as in Lidia Yuknavitch's book, *The Chronology of Water*, the Hero gets fed up with things the way things are and prepares to depart – to leave the family to fulfill her dream of a swimming scholarship.

The Magic of Synchronicity

In this phase of a story, it's sometimes beneficial to explore the magic that starts showing up during the *Call to Growth*. It can be a mysterious time as signs and messages can no longer be seen as mere coincidences. Some people may refer to this as the hand of fate and destiny, but there is a mystery when so many incidents occur that lead to us turning around, or looking up, or looking deep inside and listening to a calling that was a seed that is now sprouting – and we must pay attention to it now.

The Hero May Be Off His Game

At this point in the story perhaps a wife or husband has asked for a divorce, or an old friend might reappear to push the Hero in a new direction. This friend might or might not be trusted. In Debbie Augenthaler's book *You are Not Alone*, her husband is about to die. She has received premonitions, but pushed them aside. Often at this stage of a story, the Hero is disoriented in some way, and nothing feels quite right as they don't yet realize they are in preparation to leave behind the Old World, and move toward a New World, a new way of being.

The reason the Hero is off his game now is because the energy of what lies ahead is mixed – no change occurs without obstacles and challenges, without pain and suffering and joy. Everyone knows this – how wrenching change can be. The *Call to Growth* comes with the sounds and smells of change, and a glimpse into the adventure. It's frightening, which is why heroes first refuse the call. Our intuition knows that just beyond the call are dragons and demons and angels and cliffs, and delicious oceans, and we will walk to the edge of those cliffs and jump. Will the Hero survive? There is danger in adventure, and sometimes deep sorrow, and the *Call to Growth* can throw the Hero off their emotional foundation, while they are deciding.

It's all too much at first — both exciting and disorienting, and before we *Refuse the Call*, we must stagger in the bright rays and shield our eyes for a moment, remembering how comfortable life could be, if only the knock never came to our door, the whisper never spoke into our ear.

At this stage in the story, the Hero is listening, he is paying attention and we are absorbing.

The *Call to Growth* can come as that last moment that pushes him over the edge toward change.

A Call to Growth Can Be Tragic

It's important to remember a *Call to Growth* can be ominous in some stories. Before my boyfriend died, two psychics told me he was going to die. Many heroes have multiple warnings of danger, or dreams that serve as premonitions, or an addiction of some sort that will lead to so many obstacles.

A *Call to Growth* can be triggered by loss or grief – something may be taken away and the Hero is stripped of something precious or necessary. Perhaps the Hero has lost all his money, or his home – or he has received an unexpected medical diagnosis. Perhaps the Hero comes home and finds his wife in bed with another man, or in Debbie Augenthaler's book, *You are Not Alone*, her husband dies unexpectedly in her arms.

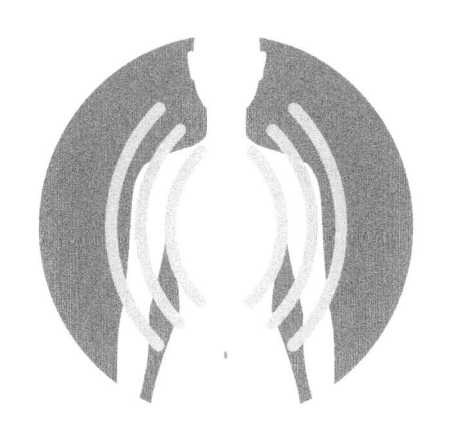

the CALL to GROWTH

LITERARY examples

Archaic Torso of Apollo
Rainer Maria Rilke, 1875 – 1926

We cannot know his legendary head
with eyes like ripening fruit. And yet his torso
is still suffused with brilliance from inside,
like a lamp, in which his gaze, now turned to low,

gleams in all its power. Otherwise
the curved breast could not dazzle you so, nor could
a smile run through the placid hips and thighs
to that dark center where procreation flared.

Otherwise this stone would seem defaced
beneath the translucent cascade of the shoulders
and would not glisten like a wild beast's fur:

would not, from all the borders of itself,
burst like a star: for here there is no place
that does not see you. You must change your life.

the CALL to GROWTH

READ

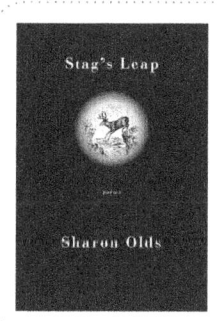

Stag's Leap

Sharon Olds

Tiny Siren Page 56
In this part of the story, she is receiving a sign that her husband might be having an affair.

The Chronology of Water

Lidia Yuknavitch

Suitcase Page 49

You Are Not Alone

Debbie Augenthaler

Those Three Words Page 1

The Color of Water

James McBride

Page 107

The past, present and future are all alive in you, waiting to be turned into story.

Laura Lentz

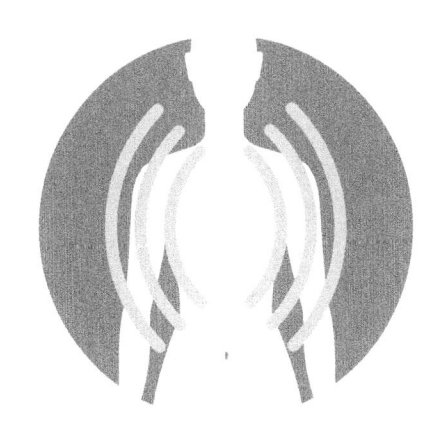

the CALL to GROWTH

create **YOUR** story

STORYlab2

Writing Warm-Ups

Two-minute warm-ups prepare you for the longer writing exercises.

Set a timer for one-minute.

Use the first sentence as a starter sentence, then write for another minute using the second sentence.

Repeat.

WRITING WARM-UP 1

Until one day...
[write for one minute]

And because of this...
[write for another minute]

WRITING WARM-UP 2

The message didn't come in a bottle.
[write for one minute]

...as if the hand of fate grabbed my wrist.
[write for another minute]

Pre-Writing Exploration
List Your Call to Growth Elements

For five minutes, make a list of Times of Change in the beginning of your story. After listing them in the column, go back and write next to it the name of a person instrumental in that change (enemy or friend). In the third column list the symbols, signs or synchronicities that showed up.

TIMES OF CHANGE

Make a list of unexpected events or thoughts that led you to consider change.
[write for five minutes]

NAME OF THE PERSON

The names of people instrumental in that change or circumstance.

SYMBOLS, SIGNS OR SYNCHRONICITIES

List symbols, signs or synchronicities that showed up during the Call to Growth.

STORYlab2

Create Your Call to Growth
Writing Instructions:

Choose the writing prompt that inspires you. Later, you can explore each prompt.

Write for thirteen minutes without stopping, or overthinking your content. Set your timer!

1 THING THAT PUSHED YOU OVER THE EDGE

Write about the one thing that pushed you over the edge toward this major change in life.
[write for 13 minutes]

2 TIME OF SYNCHRONICITY

Write about a time of synchronicity that turned out to be a Big Sign.
[write for 13 minutes]

3 THING YOU MOST FEARED

Write about the one thing you most feared if you ventured into a different life.
[write for 13 minutes]

Create Your Story
Writing Instructions:

Choose the writing prompt that inspires you. Later, you can explore each prompt.

Write for thirteen minutes without stopping, or overthinking your content. Set your timer!

1 Warning Signs

Write about the warning signs you received that it was time to change or that something big was going to happen.
[write for 13 minutes]

2 Time of Disorientation

Write about an early time of disorientation or confusion before your Call to Growth.
[write for 13 minutes]

3 Precipitating Character

Write about a character, it could be a mentor or a sinister character that precipitated your Call to Growth.
[write for 13 minutes]

"If there is a knock on your door — a call to change your life — and you don't answer the door, your door might get kicked down. If you buy a new door with dead bolt locks, your house might burn to the ground. If you don't answer your call then, you might get sick. The Universe will get your attention somehow. All you had to do was answer the door."

Laura Lentz

STORYlab3

REFUSAL of the CALL

I've been working on the railroad, all the live-long day,
I've been working on the railroad, just to pass the time away...

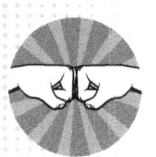

"You don't have to stay committed to something just because you're good at it."
Brittany Burgunder

"Say no to everything, so you can say yes to the one thing."
Richie Norton

"An acorn turns into an oak tree…it's extraordinary.… The difference between you and me, and the acorn, is that we can say no."
Marianne Williamson

"You're not cut out for this, Joan, and you know it."
Diane Thomas — Romancing the Stone

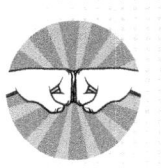

Refusal of the Call
When Dreams Are Deferred

My father could pick up any musical instrument and play it. Although he couldn't read music, he could hear each note and play along with any song — piano, drums, xylophone or saxophone. An untrained musician, the reed of any instrument was as familiar to his mouth as his own tongue. In spite of his call to express himself through music, he stayed in his cubicle at the phone company for the sake of supporting his family. But what happens when dreams are deferred? What happens when we don't answer our call?

When our dreams are knocking on our door, and we look at them through the peephole, and then go back to our lives before we heard the knocking, it's a dangerous path. We aren't meant to live in fear or to live our lives with less joy. The Universe wants you to take chances - it wants you to risk and give up security for a bigger dream of stepping into your true self.

And yet, in every story — and throughout history — the Hero refuses the call at first. She turns away from the knock on the door, the signs leading her heart in its true direction for the security of what she knows.

Often, in this phase of the STORYquest, the main character will find themselves a victim of the circumstances of the *World of Before*, the familiar world — needing to be saved, not understanding the only way to save themselves is by opening Pandora's Box. My father was a "victim" of his family - supporting his children, with a wife who kept him from his dreams because she saw them as a threat.

This doesn't mean the Hero isn't successful — she may be refusing her call while building a successful empire. However, whatever empire she builds, it will be an empire where the grim reaper is just around the corner. When we are hiding inside a world we know we should leave behind, God or The Universe creates new, bigger problems, and we know deep down we are awaiting the gradual approach where everything crumbles and falls apart.

Refusal of the Call — Don't Go!!

Christopher Vogler writes, "Almost always, the Hero initially balks at the call. He or she is being asked to face the greatest of all fears, the terrible unknown. This hesitation signals the reader that the adventure is risky, the stakes are high, and the Hero could lose fortune or life." I have always told my friends if you don't answer your call, you are risking your body becoming ill, and if you continue to not answer your call, The Universe might just take your life, forcing you to start over because you are so far off track.

The reader likes to see the Hero hesitant before answering their true calling, because the reader can relate to this phase of the Hero's Quest. Writing about overcoming fear and reluctance makes the story intriguing. The more the refusal, the deeper the heels of your character are dug into the earth, refusing to go. The reader witnesses the character being worn down to finally succumbing and saying yes.

The Hero's inner voice becomes doubtful the Hero should change. This inner voice also serves to warn the reader that she may not succeed on this adventure, which is always more interesting than a sure thing. A story that is a sure thing doesn't hold the reader's interest. In literature, there is often a friend or a parent who is the voice of reason and caution — encouraging the Hero to stay safe where they are, to not take the risk.

SUMMARY: Refusal of the Call

- Sense of duty or obligation to family, work or friends

- Avoidance

- Fear

- Inability to handle all that lies ahead in the journey

- Insecurity

- Life's Distractions

REFUSAL of the CALL

LITERARY examples

STORYlab3

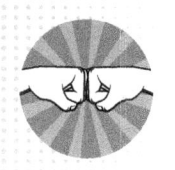

READ

Refusal of the call shows up in many different configurations in literature. In Sharon Olds' poem *Gramercy*, she makes love to her husband, who has proclaimed he is leaving. In Debbie Augenthaler's book, *You Are Not Alone*, she has resumed the routine of daily life, but gives up one winter night after arriving home from work to a dark and empty house. In *The Color of Water*, James McBride takes us on a hilarious romp on his mother's decision making to relocate her family from Harlem to Delaware.

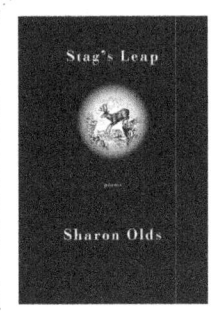

Stag's Leap
Sharon Olds
Gramercy Page 9

You Are Not Alone
Debbie Augenthaler
Chapter Seven

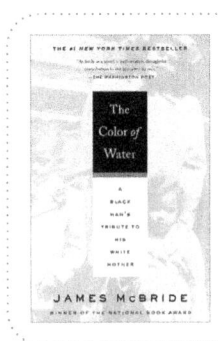

The Color of Water
James McBride
Chapter Eighteen

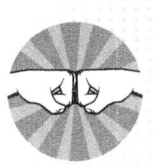

REFUSAL of the CALL

My Refusal
Laura Lentz

I had grown weary of my own success and it stopped feeling like success and instead felt like a burden. Somewhere along the way—between the airports and hotels and meeting preparations, between hiring and firing and building successful programs for my clients, my clients stopped caring about the programs I built making a difference in the community.

Despite the awards. Despite the increase in brand share for my clients, I was unsteady in my career path.

To save money, the Fortune 500 companies fired all of their senior marketing people. And to save more money, they asked us to build programs they could hand over to someone else who would do them cheaper.

I didn't understand until I got very sick that it was time to let go of that life and that I was ignoring all the signs. And after I got very sick, I turned my business over to my capable employees for a while, because I was told by doctors I was going to die anyway.

But then I didn't die.

During that time away from from business - during my break - I saw angels and healers from the future. I had a toe in the cold water of change, and then my foot. The problem was that the rest of my body was still straddling my old life.

St. Benedict said "when ready for major change, pray for guidance, and then make your decision. Then live your decision fully without question and do not look back. It's in looking back that one initiates profound suffering."

But knowing this, I went back to work to engage with my old life after inviting the music back into my soul. Because after inviting the music back in, I didn't die. After seeing Broadway plays and jazz shows, museums and Esalen, I began to remember life.

I remembered how to breathe again.

After I returned to my old life, the music faded. I couldn't even hear the orchestra tuning.

I couldn't figure out the weird cash flow at my company, and one day I went to work and my accountant and one of my project managers had something to tell me behind closed doors—one of my managers had been stealing money.

For a long time.

They called the police, and I called him into my office with the evidence while we were waiting for the police and he said he was sorry, so sorry. And maybe he cried.

STORYlab3

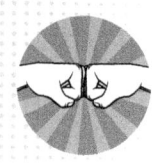

I stood up from behind my big expensive desk with the metal and wood in my designer clothes and I went to him - this man I had trusted to take care of things—and I took his face between my hands, his round face like the full moon, and I kissed his forehead.

I said, "Thank you." Because that day I had to put the rest of my body into the water and jump in. I had to stop refusing my call.

I left that life. I was done Refusing the Call. And I came to an island in the middle of the Pacific Ocean.

If I told you, "From that day forward, life was easy," I would be lying. I had obstacles and challenges and hurdles and when I got over them, The Universe challenged me again.

But I knew better than to look back.

And today I am writing this story to remind you of this: when The Universe knocks on your door with a message and you don't answer it, it will kick your door down and come inside. If you ignore it then, it might burn your house down. While you are standing looking at the ash and rubble—and you continue to ignore the messages, The Universe just might just turn your life upside down and reset you.

This story is a warning: Don't ignore your calling.

Move toward it every day.

Put your toe in the water of change. Then up to your knee, then jump in already. The water will be so cold at first, and the current strong. It will take you away from all that is familiar, and you will feel like you are drowning.

Do it anyway.

Do what feeds your soul or you will experience total chaos, and the chaos will get worse until you can't even hear one note.

Not even middle C.

But once you start to listen, everything will get better and I promise you the whole orchestra will return.

But first you have to open your door.

Go ahead.

Answer it.

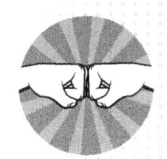

REFUSAL of the CALL

create YOUR story

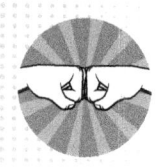

Writing Warm-Ups

Two-minute warm-ups prepare you for the longer writing exercises.

Set a timer for one-minute.

Use the first sentence as a starter sentence, then write for another minute using the second sentence.

Repeat.

WRITING WARM-UP 1

They asked me not to go.
[write for one minute]

The stakes were high.
[write for another minute]

WRITING WARM-UP 2

I opened Pandora's box.
[write for one minute]

Even though I was told never.
[write for another minute]

REFUSAL of the CALL

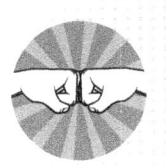

Create Your Story — Conflicting Calls

Many years ago, I came to Kauaʻi for love, and thought I had fallen in love with a man, but I had fallen in love with a place. By insisting my love was for the man and not Kauaʻi, I was refusing my call to a much richer life. Sometimes, we have conflicting calls, or conflicting magnets luring us to growth. The direction may be right, but we choose it for all the wrong reasons initially. I came to Kauaʻi for all the wrong reasons to find the right life for me.

Writing Instructions:

Choose the writing prompt that inspires you. Later, you can explore each prompt. Write for thirteen minutes without stopping, or overthinking your content. Set your timer!

1 YOU AVOIDED THE CALL

Write about a Call to Growth and all the ways you avoided it.
[write for 13 minutes]

2 CALAMITY

Write about the calamity in your life that happened when you Refused a Call.
[write for 13 minutes]

3 TALK YOU OUT OF SOMETHING

Write about a person that tried to talk you out of something you thought was good for you — and what transpired as a result of that conversation.
[write for 13 minutes]

4 WISHED YOU HAD REFUSED

Write about a Call to Growth that you wish you had refused at first and why.
[write for 13 minutes]

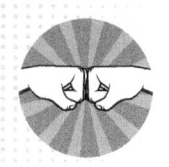

The Familiar World will cling to you like a vine

When you are getting ready to undertake a major change in your life, or a great adventure, The *World of Before* knows, and clings to you. It sings its sweetest, most insistent song, a lullaby to lull you back into your most comforting place you have ever known. Countless distractions tempt you off track, including love, puppies, a great job offer — even a perfect place to live by a babbling brook with baby birds in a nest outside your bedroom window. It's as if The Universe is testing you, to see if you are worthy of the adventure, of becoming the Hero. Are you willing to sacrifice the gold and jewels The Universe may be laying in your path to distract you?

Refusal may also be an opportunity to redirect your focus. An adventure taken on a whim or to escape some unpleasant consequence may be nudged into a deeper adventure of the spirit.

If your *Call to Growth* is part of a Grief Story, this may be the time when you have trouble accepting your fate – your life without the person you loved.

Why Your Story Needs the Hero to Hesitate

- You will inform the reader that the challenges ahead are so enormous.

- The reader will feel the stakes and understand them. A part of the reader will want you to stay!

- You want the reader to feel and experience your fear and hesitation. The reader is risking everything with you.

REFUSAL of the CALL

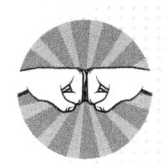

Create Your Story
Writing Instructions:

Choose the writing prompt that inspires you. Later, you can explore each prompt.

Write for thirteen minutes without stopping, or overthinking your content. Set your timer!

1 AVOIDANCE

Write about a time you clung to something to avoid taking the next step of your journey.
[write for 13 minutes]

2 THE LURE

Write about all the things that showed up for you when you were getting ready to change – What lured you to stay.
[write for 13 minutes]

3 WHAT'S AT STAKE?

Write about all that is at stake when you open the door to change everything, everything you will lose.
[write for 13 minutes]

I was so blessed.
The first person
I gave all my heart to
was an angel
who plucked the feathers
off his wings
and built a nest.

Kamand Kojouri

STORYlab4

MENTORS & ANGELS

The wisdom of the guide

"Like the cotton-carder who combs tangled cotton into a long bundle of fibre, you take all my knotted fragments and comb them into light."

Kamand Kojouri

"I am not a teacher, but an awakener."

Robert Frost

"We're here for a reason. I believe a bit of the reason is to throw little torches out to lead people through the dark."

Whoopi Goldberg

"Mentors change lives, but students change mentors' lives more."

Richie Norton

"The role of most leaders is to get the people to think more of the leader, but the role of the exceptional leader is to get people to think more of themselves."

Booker T. Washington

"A mentor is someone who allows you to see the hope inside yourself."

Oprah Winfrey

The Wisdom of the Guide
The Deep Bond Between Mentor & Hero

The Mentor represents the bond between parent and child, teacher and student, doctor and patient, god and man, even friend and dog! The mentor prepares the Hero to face the unknown, to accept the adventure that is calling to him.

We have all had mentors in our lives, and our mentors change as our lives change. In the stories we write, the mentor can be the glue that holds the Hero together and pushes them on their inevitable adventure. The Mentor can be the one person that shows the Hero what he needs to stop refusing his life calling.

This is the point in a story when The Mentor usually shows up — when the ordinary world is breaking apart by the *Call to Growth* and the Hero is frozen. The Hero's toe is in the vast ocean, testing the water — and the mentor lightly pushes the Hero off balance so he can finally go tumbling down into the icy water of change.

Often the Mentor is already known to the Hero and may have been offering advice and giving subtle nudges from the start. It's the Mentor's job to help the Hero prepare for the journey ahead. They may offer guidance, or equipment, or just the sharp push the Hero needs to get them moving.

A Mentor Can Be a Critical Character

Your story may not have a Mentor as a main character, but instead a series of mentors. This chapter is to help you discover if a Mentor will be an essential part of your story — and how not to overlook the opportunity to pull a Mentor in as a main character. I call Mentors that come and go throughout a book our angels.

It is common for a Mentor to train the Hero, but sometimes the Mentor will make an enormous sacrifice —occasionally with their life. If this is the case, the Hero moves forward with the enormous sacrifice made on his behalf, and uses that sacrifice to fuel his actions into the unknown with faith and on the wings of sacrifice of a beloved.

The Mentor may also serve as an external conscience for the protagonist, designed to point out and guide the Hero. He attempts to keep the Hero on the path designed for him. So, think of the Mentor as a life coach, assisting in the mission and the mindset of the Hero. Could the Mentor arrive for the Hero in a series of flashbacks? Absolutely!

Writing the Mentor

When writing in the Mentor character into any genre of any story, writers must be careful of the following:

1. The Mentor is a believable character.

2. The Mentor doesn't become a cliché. - in other words, don't make the Mentor the perfect person - it's important to show us their humanity.

3. Flawed characters are more compelling to watch and ring truer for your reader, so make sure to show the reader the flaws of your Mentor — maybe they save lives every day but smoke at the end of the day — maybe they teach you about relationship but their own marriage is falling apart.

Like Heroes, Mentors may be willing or unwilling. Sometimes they teach in spite of themselves. In other cases they teach by their bad example. The downfall of a weakened, flawed Mentor can show the Hero pitfalls to avoid. As with Heroes, all characters have shadow sides, including angels.

Considerations for Writing a Mentor into a Book:

- Mentors are the Hero's conscience and teacher - Like a GPS.

- They motivate the Hero.

- Initiate the Hero into the mysterious.

- Throw the Hero a torch in the dark.

- Gifts that Mentors bestow on their groups should be earned.

- Mentors motivate the Hero and help her overcome fear — help the Hero commit to the adventure.

- Mentors "plant" seeds of information that reveal themselves later in the story.

Most Common Archetypes of Mentors:

Fallen Mentors

This is one of the most interesting types of Mentors, and this Mentor might be on a Hero's journey of their own. Mostly they are experiencing a crisis of faith in their own calling, but within the layers of their own crisis, Fallen Mentors are often on a Hero's Journey of their own. They are fallen and the Hero needs the Mentor to pull themselves together one more time to help them.

Coffee Mentor

These are often recurring characters in a story. A Coffee mentor is someone you connect with regularly in a cafe, in the break room at work, or at a monthly dinner. They may be your house cleaner or your UPS delivery person. Their role is to offer advice and a sounding board – and they stay interwoven throughout the story.

Comic Mentor

They come in the form of Hero sidekicks, giving advice that seems wrong in the beginning, but often turns out to be the perfect solution in the end. They can make the Hero laugh when she wants to cry, or see the tragedy through a new lens.

Mystical Mentor

This is a leader, a medicine man, a medicine woman — they are life guides, traveling to other worlds in dreams and visions and returning with stories to enlighten their tribes. Mystical Mentors can also be Earth Angels, though we never see their wings.

Writing is finding the courage to discover and embrace your truth, and then become the master of that truth.

Laura Lentz

MENTORS & ANGELS

LITERARY examples

Mentors Straddle The Shadows

Years ago my neighbor's husband taught me how to speak by teaching me how to read. Nobody knew why I wouldn't talk, and I don't remember not talking. I do recall the details of the afternoon under the maple tree in a rusted white lawn chair, me sitting in his lap with an open book. Russ teaching me the sounds of the alphabet and how to put those sounds together until I was reading. Reading out loud taught me to speak, and the whole world opened to me that afternoon.

Russ also taught me how to swim, throw a hardball and navigate my complex family. He brought other teachers to me, including a rabbi who had been buried alive in the holocaust, and taught me about grief. Looking back, Russ was my first mentor. He often took me to a public pool in Wildwood, New Jersey. The woman checking our membership tags told him he had a lovely daughter - and he just said *thank you*.

Like many Mentors, he was broken, and when I was nine years old I learned he had two wives — my mother's best friend next door and another wife in the city and a daughter with the other wife. I felt betrayed, and my mother insisted I no longer see him. But we sometimes met in secret at the white wooden fence separating our yards when my mother was working. He remained "married" to both his wives until he died.

If I were to place this character in my memoir or turn him into a fictional character, it would be a rich exploration — because all mentors are human, and all humans straddle the shadows. A mentor may offer critical teachings and advice, but have a difficult time living up to their own teachings.

Mentors often show up in a side story in a surprising way, and help the Hero to grow. They provide aid, advice, and sometimes magic to get the Hero out of a jam — or they provide the Hero another way of thinking that will help her on her long journey.

Mentors are critical to every story, because nobody is on a journey alone — we must learn our lessons from someone or something that happens to us.

Mentors inspire the Hero to rise, making a personal learning from a mentor a universal experience for the reader.

To this day, I don't open a book, read a poem or write a story without thinking of the thick hands of the first man I loved in the rusted lawn chair, opening the whole world to me through the world of story.

READ

My all time favorite mentor shows up in Joel ben Izzy's book *The Beggar King and the Secret of Happiness*. If you have a mentor as a major character in your book, I highly recommend reading Joel's entire book and studying the way his mentor shows up. Lenny shows up as a Fallen Mentor, a Shaman, a Comic Mentor, and he also becomes a sacrifice for Joel's journey. This delightful book is a perfect example of a mentor who becomes the GPS that guides the Hero often through his own flaws and also holds the story together. Lenny shows up in the prologue, but when he shows up in the story in Chapter Four, we are swept along into the relationship.

The Beggar King and the Secret of Happiness

Joel ben Izzy

Chapter Four

I Was an Earth Angel
Laura Lentz

One spring morning, a man fell 25 feet out of a mango tree near my bedroom window and the sound of his body hitting the ground woke me. Followed by the kind of scream you never want to hear again. It rattled the stones in my driveway.

Stories often don't start out good – someone draws a gun, grabs a child out of a river, crashes their car into a pole and then their whole life changes, and a new story begins.

He couldn't stand up, because his hip bones were no longer where they belonged and every time he tried to stand, he fell over. Three of us were with him. We kept telling him to get back down. To stay down.

I called an ambulance. The ambulance didn't come.

I called again and they said they were with a dead woman in Hanalei (twenty minutes away), and I walked past the fence so the man on the ground couldn't hear me, and I said "for FUCK sake can you please choose this man who is still alive? And go back for the dead person later?"

More than thirty minutes after this man hit the ground, the ambulance arrived, and we were still forty minutes from Wilcox hospital.

He said he wanted me to go with him in the ambulance. I had been holding his hand, talking with him. I don't remember what I said.

The mango branch that he sawed off and knocked him out of the tree was beside us. The ambulance driver said you can't ride in the back while they put him on a stretcher, so I rode in the front.

The hospital is forty minutes from Kilauea. I could tell by the calls to the hospital in the ambulance that his vitals weren't good. Halfway to Kapa'a I asked why they hadn't given him pain meds yet. He called me his angel. I didn't feel like an angel, I felt like someone who woke up too early to a man falling out of a tree. I kept lying to him we were almost there, that everything would be alright.

When we arrived, he wouldn't let go of my hand, and from that moment on the staff let me into his room, assuming I was his wife.

What can I do to help? I said amid the chaos and shouting or nurse to doctor and doctor to nurse.

Cut off his shorts, a nurse said, handing me scissors, and so I did, and as I peeled them off, I yelled. *He's bleeding!* More shouts and bags of blood and chaos, and that's when his heart stopped.

They pulled out the equipment and told me to go the top of his bed and yell his name. His eyes were closed. In the middle of the chaos of the electric paddles and his chest lifting into the air, I yelled his name three times.

He had leaves and dirt on his face.

His heart began beating again, and he opened his eyes, and they continued working on him to stabilize him. And then his heart stopped again, only this time for longer, and the equipment again, and his chest lifting again, and me yelling his name again.

He opened his eyes and he looked into my eyes like he had seen something.

I bent over. *Listen to me,* I said loudly into his left ear. *Do you want to live or are you ready to die?* I felt the whole room was waiting for his answer.

He said without hesitation – *I want to live.*

Then tell your heart, because your heart has stopped twice. Tell your heart you want to live.

His heart heard him, and I went outside, because now that he was talking with his body, I felt he didn't need me. By now the *Sons of Kaua'i* were gathering in solidarity on their bikes; I gave them the update. They were praying. His daughter came.

They prepared a helicopter to Oahu and the daughter handed me her son so she could join her father. The boy was six or seven at the time and his mother said Aunty, can you drive him to his grandma's? And I drove that small boy to his grandma's and went home exhausted.

In these uncertain medical times, please don't forget you can talk to your body anytime and tell it you want to live. Words are better than vitamin C. Strengthen your immune system with them. Breathe well, eat well, tell your body what you want it to know. Gather your organs as soldiers on your battlefield.

The man who fell out of the tree survived because he wanted to live, but he was gone for a long time. When he returned to Kaua'i, months later, he called me his angel.

In our stories and in our lives, we always wait for angels to show up to add the magic, but they are always there, shadowing us. We ARE each other's angels. We always have each other.

I know this man didn't fall out of a tree by my bedroom window by accident five years ago. In the end he saved his own life.

I just reminded him how.

*Stories can conquer fear, you know.
They can make the heart bigger.*

Ben Okri

MENTORS & ANGELS

createYOURstory

STORYlab4

Writing Warm-Ups

Two-minute warm-ups prepare you for the longer writing exercises.

Set a timer for one-minute.

Use the first sentence as a starter sentence, then write for another minute using the second sentence.

Repeat.

WRITING WARM-UP 1

They threw a torch to me in the dark.
[write for one minute]

She said, "you're here for a reason."
[write for another minute]

WRITING WARM-UP 2

I stood on your shoulders so I could see.
[write for one minute]

He handed it to me like a magic sword.
[write for another minute]

MENTORS & ANGELS

Pre-Writing Exploration
Who is Your Mentor?

Think of one of the main mentors in your story.

Write their name at the top of the page.

Pre-Writing Instructions:

Complete each of these three exercises, writing for two minutes on each.

1 Deeply Human

List attributes that make your mentor deeply human.
[write for 2 minutes]

2 Gifts & Magic

List the gifts and magic you were given by your mentor.
[write for 2 minutes]

3 How Those Gifts Helped

Write how those gifts helped you in your journey.
[write for 2 minutes]

STORYlab4

Create Your Story
Writing Instructions:

Choose the writing prompt that inspires you. Later, you can explore each prompt.

Write for thirteen minutes without stopping, or overthinking your content. Set your timer!

1 PUSHED INTO THE CALL

Write about a mentor that pushed you into your Call to Growth and how their guidance made you take that final step.
[write for 13 minutes]

2 UNLIKELY MENTOR

Imagine a mentor at a time in your life who was the most unlikely mentor —maybe they smoked cigarettes or couldn't get their own life together, but somehow they were able to help you.
[write for 13 minutes]

3 CONSISTANT MENTOR

Write about a mentor who keeps showing up for you, as your journey shape shifts and you have new obstacles in your path.
[write for 13 minutes]

4 PARENT AS MENTOR

Tell a story of a parent or parent figure who behaved as a mentor at one point in your journey.
[write for 13 minutes]

Inner Mentors

The Mentor Hero

- In some stories, there is no Mentor or guide. The Hero has become his own mentor as he lives within his own ethical and moral code of behavior.

- A Mentor can come up in memory and not be a living person

- The Hero's Mentor lives inside of him as a strong inner part of self, sometimes coming up in internal dialogue.

- An inner Mentor might have a gift or artifact from another time – from ancestors that they use as an outer guide to ignite the inner mentor.

The Inner Mentor

Author Tara Mohr talks about those rare moments in our lives when we have a clear, wise intuition or thought, and we see the solution. We have those moments here or there, but we can't easily access that part of ourselves consistently.

The "inner mentor" is a tool that allows us to access that wisest part of ourselves much more reliably.

In story, the inner mentor can come up as an inner character or alter ego:

The inner mentor is the voice Elizabeth Gilbert hears in *Eat, Pray, Love* when she is sobbing on the floor of her bathroom in the middle of the night. It tells her, "Go to bed, Liz." In Debbie Augenthaler's book, *You are Not Alone*, it's the voice that speaks to her in her lowest moment of grief.

In part we are more familiar with the inner critic than the inner mentor because we hear the inner critic voice more loudly. The inner critic demands our attention. The inner mentor waits to be paid attention to. Where the inner critic rants and raves, the inner mentor speaks softly. The inner critic interrupts and invades our thinking. The inner mentor almost always waits to be asked for input before she speaks.

STORYlab4

Create Your Story
Writing Instructions:

Choose the writing prompt that inspires you. Later, you can explore each prompt.

Write for thirteen minutes without stopping, or overthinking your content. Set your timer!

1 THE RIGHT MOMENT

Write about a time when your Inner Mentor or Earth Angel showed up to guide you at just the right moment for just the right path.
[write for 13 minutes]

2 SHOWING UP

What are the qualities of your Inner Mentor and show us all the ways she shows up to keep you going.
[write for 13 minutes]

3 DAILY LIFE

Describe your inner mentor as a major character—tell us all the details about how she eats and spends her time, as if her daily life is very different from your daily life.
[write for 13 minutes]

4 GUIDED BY YOUR FUTURE SELF

Write a letter to your self today from your future self in ten years, offering you guidance that you need to hear right now.
[write for 13 minutes]

Broken Wing
Wendi Romero

It didn't stop the caterpillar
from crawling on its belly
nor did it keep it from
curling, not knowing that it
would hang upside down
for days in the dark.
It didn't stop the butterfly
from taking to flight
nor did it keep a clipped
wing from laboring against
a hard shell to break
through its long night.
Not knowing imperfection
or limitations, off it flew
broken wing and all.

*Broken Wing from **Reflections of the Heart** ©2018 by Wendi Romero. Reprinted with permission of Wendi Romero.*

STORYlab5

JUMPING into the PORTAL

Leaving your old world behind

STORYlab5

"He had the vague sense of standing on a threshold, the crossing of which would change everything."
Kate Morton — The Forgotten Garden

"Confidence comes from crossing thresholds."
Kamal Ravikant — Live Your Truth

"In The Universe, there are things that are known, and things that are unknown, and in between them, there are doors."
William Blake

"I walked up the stairs and hesitated at the open door."
Susan Hill — The Small Hand

Jumping into the Portal
One Foot in The New World, One in The Old World

At this point in your story, the Hero is about to embark on the Quest, whether it be physical, spiritual or emotional — she is fully committed and ready to leave the familiar *World of Before* behind. She leaves behind everything she knows — friends, family, and most importantly — an old way of moving through the world. Mary Oliver, in her poem *The Journey* writes, "the whole house began to tremble and you felt the old tug at your ankles."

When the Hero is at this place, she will feel the tug of those she loves — all that binds her to an old, familiar life and other world.

It's difficult to turn her back on this and pull away from the familiar, but she has made her decision and is ready to go.

Where is the Hero now? Between the old and the new, with one foot moving to leave and one still planted in the *World of Before*. The reader knows the growth has begun, for good or for whatever challenges and obstacles lie ahead.

The Hero's Soul is at Stake

In this part of the story, Heroes come to a decision point where their very souls are at stake. When I closed my marketing company in Los Angeles and made the decision to commit to life on Kaua'i and a new career, I had one foot in my old world and one foot in my new world. When I finally relocated to Kaua'i, the decision was easy. If I stayed in Los Angeles, a part of me would have died.

At this point in our journey, we must ask of our Hero — does she go on living her life as she always has, or will she risk everything to grow and change?

This part of the story involves a very big Leap of Faith. Does she go on with her life the way it is, or take the leap.

The Barricade

Before the Hero takes off to the other side, there will be people ready to bounce her back, setting up barricades to keep him from crossing. Mary Oliver writes in her poem *The Journey*, "and the road was full of branches and stones". In *Eat, Pray, Love*, Elizabeth Gilbert felt her husband and their attorneys were keeping the divorce papers from moving forward to signature, blocking her from her new life.

STORYlab5

The task for the writer is to have the Hero find a solution – a way around the person who set up the barricade.

The person blocking your entrance to your new life might turn out to be a mentor or an earth angel in the end.

JUMPING into the PORTAL

LITERARY examples

Instructions for the Journey
Laura Lentz

Before you go,
give everything away
to someone who is staying,
someone whose job
is to hold down the fort,
fold the sheets,
light the candle, and also
blow the candle out.

Take the socks off so your feet
remember the earth.

Don't fly – you'll miss the valleys,
the abandoned cars,
the Indians, the coyotes.
The intersections and the signs,
the rutted road,
the toothless man pumping your gas.

Drive across the landscape slowly.
Look into the next car
and see the small child
who never sucked her thumb
but holds books in her hands
the whole alphabet stuck to her fingers.

Drive all of who you are –
the mother, the queen, the orphan
through Tennessee and New Mexico
to the unmoving freeways
of southern California
where orange groves once bloomed.

Bury your memories into the same soil
your mother loved, let your fingers
hold the bulbs she held,
even the one that never bloomed.
Peer into the Over of all life
while you're still on your knees.

Then, sleep on the ground anywhere.
Find Venus, Jupiter, the Big Dipper.
Know the moon is tucked behind
the one small cloud,
inviting you to remember the sun.

When morning comes, the Albatross
will be slapping their beaks to love.
You will wake to that sound,
the clouds now gone, your body drying
from last night's storm.

Now you know this:
Your mother's garden will always be there,
you don't have to dig.
You are the bulb she delivered
back to the earth.
You are the bloom.

©2020 by Laura Lentz

The Initiation
Laura Lentz

For all the Aloha, Kauaʻi was the most unwelcoming place I had ever visited, except for Paris, France and Houston, Texas. The local girls wouldn't serve me a drink at the Tahiti Nui and the mainland women gave me side-eye and tucked their husbands into their purses when I walked by.

It wasn't because I was a Haole (one without breath); I didn't understand that I hadn't yet been initiated and therefore did not belong. I was straddling two worlds—going back and forth between Los Angeles and Kauaʻi—afraid to just go forth. I wore the "back" of back and forth on my skin, clinging to an old life. I had given up nothing to live here.

My real initiation was to come.

I had to lose almost everything until I was only going forth, and during this time, my daughter started to disappear from me, eating only blocks of lettuce and sometimes a leaf of kale, and running fifteen miles a day, down the dirt road to Larson's Beach and over the rocks, and more lettuce, pushing other food like avocado and macadamia nuts to the edge of the plate because of the fat.

When we practiced yoga together, people stared at me — the mother — as if to say *do something*. Her shoulder blades began to look like wings. They didn't know I was shadowing her and fighting for her silently. Carrying her disappearing body so gently in my cupped hands, putting her small beating heart on my own pillow at night and talking to it, though she was sleeping in another room.

I sang the sweetest lullaby only a mother can quietly sing to a suffering teenaged girl, hoping the notes reached her in her darkest night.

I was straddling two worlds and afraid to jump fully into one. I was the marketing executive, though I began writing groups and editing. My daughter was familiar with the back and forth, she spent her whole life straddling two worlds — mine and her father's.

We often forget the people we love are being initiated too, and their pain parallels our pain and sometimes intersects. In this way, we are all initiating each other, holding space for each other's dark, and celebrating each other's beaming, shooting stars. Going back and forth with each other until we are just going forth.

While some stars are being born, others go out. Sometimes we are just a low flickering candle, and sometimes the wind blows our light out for a period of time. Both my daughter and I were trying to find our way then, and we both did find our way. She started eating. What had been taken from her — the list was long. What had been taken from me — the list was long.

JUMPING into the PORTAL

And in this way, we were both initiated into the island of Kaua'i. We gave so much up to walk into our new lives.

We just had to stop looking back.

READ

The Beggar King and the Secret of Happiness

Joel ben Izzy

The Border Guard
folk tale before Chapter Six

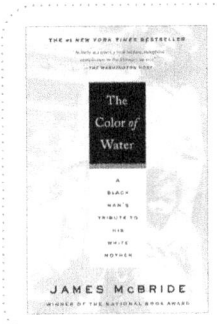

The Color of Water

James McBride

Pages 89 to 91

Stag's Leap

Sharon Olds

Approaching Godthab
page 39

STORYlab5

"Years ago a woman in Los Angeles wanted to work with me on her book, but each time it was time for us to talk, she had something come up. Finally we had scheduled a day, and ten minutes before the meeting she texted me, 'I'm so sorry, I have to go to San Diego to pick up a puppy.' There will always be a puppy, a lover, a trip we have to take, a doctor's appointment or another project – so many ways to avoid our true calling."

Laura Lentz

JUMPING into the PORTAL

create**YOUR**story

Writing Warm-Ups

Two-minute warm-ups prepare you for the longer writing exercises.

Set a timer for one-minute.

Use the first sentence as a starter sentence, then write for another minute using the second sentence.

Repeat.

WRITING WARM-UP 1

Everything was at risk.
[write for one minute]

I was stuck between two worlds.
[write for another minute]

WRITING WARM-UP 2

I began to fly, unaware I had wings.
[write for one minute]

In each word, there burned a wick.
[write for another minute]

JUMPING into the **PORTAL**

Create Your Story
Writing Instructions:

Choose the writing prompt that inspires you. Later, you can explore each prompt.

Write for thirteen minutes without stopping, or overthinking your content. Set your timer!

1 STEPPING INTO ANOTHER WORLD

*Write about a transition time of leaving one world
and getting ready to step into another.*
[write for 13 minutes]

2 THE UNWILLING HERO

*Write about your Hero being unwilling to step into the Growth,
and how that affected the crossing.*
[write for 13 minutes]

3 WHAT IS THE HERO LEAVING BEHIND

*By Jumping into the Portal, show us what the Hero is leaving behind
—perhaps grieving the old world while flying toward the new world.*
[write for 13 minutes]

4 NOTHING COULD STOP YOU

*Write about a time you suddenly knew you had to change course
and nothing could stop you.*
[write for 13 minutes]

STORYlab5

READ

In Lidia Yuknavitch's gripping memoir, her father is the person who set up a blockade for her leaving for college. Though she never tells you he was sexually abusive in the book, this chapter offers an eerie confirmation. This scene is a perfect example of the barricade a Hero must overcome to be able to continue on her quest.

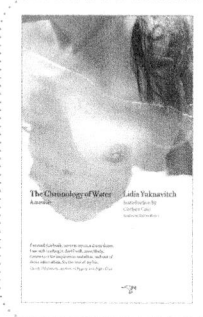

The Chronology of Water

Lidia Yuknavitch

Suitcase Chapter, page 49

JUMPING into the PORTAL

Create Your Story
Writing Instructions:

Choose the writing prompt that inspires you. Later, you can explore each prompt.

Write for thirteen minutes without stopping, or overthinking your content. Set your timer!

1 Ways Someone Made it Difficult

Describe all the ways someone made it difficult for you to cross into your Quest.
[write for 13 minutes]

2 Who Blocked Your Way

Write about a person who blocked your way and how you overcame them.
[write for 13 minutes]

3 Perspective

Tell us why someone didn't want you to go.
[write for 13 minutes]

4 Enemy Who Turned into a Friend

Write about someone who seemed like an enemy but then turned into a friend later.
[write for 13 minutes]

"[Saint Anthony] said, in his solitude, he sometimes encountered devils who looked like angels, and other times he found angels who looked like devils. When asked how he could tell the difference, the saint said that you can only tell which is which by the way you feel after the creature has left your company."

Elizabeth Gilbert — Eat, Pray, Love

STORYlab6

PUT to the TEST

Initiations

STORYlab6

"Nobody's perfect. We're all just one step up from the beasts and one step down from the angels."
Jeannette Walls — Half Broke Horses

"The nearer the dawn, the darker the night."
Henry Wadsworth Longfellow

"Anyone who has ever become anything worth writing home about has had to handle fire and brimstone with naked hands, wander in the wilderness and survive under severe limitations."
Saidi Mdala, Know What Matters

"Battling wolves today strengthens you for battling lions tomorrow."
Matshona Dhliwayo

Put to the Test

At this point in the journey, you are far from anything familiar. As with Debbie Augenthaler in *You are Not Alone*, home becomes a very different place now that her husband is gone, and Sharon Olds' world takes new navigation with the dissolution of her marriage in *Stag's Leap*.

Whether you are voluntarily going, or your journey has been forced upon you, all seekers are in a kind of shock — some seekers have a strange mix of shock with elation and trepidation. Metaphorically, your new world may feel disoriented. You have to learn a new way of doing things as you study the world around you — everything is different.

You Have Taken the Leap

The biggest difference is you have taken a leap, and now you are seeing everything through a different lens. In mythology, this would be when strange creatures jump out at you testing you, or when you are handed a meal with poison. It's time to concentrate, because your skills are about to be tested, and in these tests and trials, the Hero will come closer to all that she seeks.

Now the writer must begin to trust the journey. Trust that your character is on the right path. No different from delivering an important package to the post office, you must trust in the destination, and the many hands that package will encounter so it will arrive, where it needs to go.

At the same time, this is an important time to recognize not only your enemies, but distinguish them from the angels, because angels come in strange packages. Some enemies are put in your path just so you can learn a final lesson, and other enemies become angels.

The writing exploration ahead is all about trials, trust and judgment of character. Here the Hero is learning to become a good judge of character, an essential skill to moving forward. New friends — I call them Earth Angels — will emerge in your new world to help you navigate all the trials ahead.

Who Can Be Trusted?

Is the Hero a good judge of character? One of the tests is learning who can be trusted and relied upon and who is not be be trusted. To make the journey work, the Hero has to become an impeccable judge of character.

Most likely you will find new friends in your new world to help you navigate.

STORYlab6

Trials... Remember This:

- The Hero is getting ready to survive a succession of trials.

- This is a favorite phase of the Hero's journey in mythology and stories of adventure. This stage of the journey has produced a world of literature, and begins the gripping part of a story when you can't put the story down.

- The Hero is aided by the advice of Earth Angels who might give them a crystal, or a poem — something to guide them now. These are helpers to help the Hero navigate his New World.

- The Hero recognizes for the first time there is a certain power supporting them through this complex passage.

- This is only the beginning of the long and often perilous path of Initiations.

- Metaphorically, dragons present themselves to be conquered and surprising barriers must be passed by the Hero over and over, each one teaching a lesson.

- Throughout, the Hero glimpses the flowering gardens, the surprising gifts and small victories, all fueling them toward their ultimate destination and journey.

PUT to the TEST

LITERARY examples

Out of the Silence
Virginia Beck

You wear your body proudly
A lion in the sand…
And Life's a desire
You call your own
As it trembles under your hand.

You hear the future
Call your name,
Still growing on the tree—
 And all your fiercest loving
Cannot set you free.

You carry laughter lightly
A bird that longs to sing.
A silken cord
About its neck,
And dust,
Upon its wings.

Remember a sound
Like silence,
Falling from the stars,
Then, somewhere,
Deep inside you…
You'll hear
The bending
Of the bars.

©2019 permission by author

READ

The Chronology of Water

Lidia Yuknavitch

Deliverance: Page 57

The Color of Water

James McBride

Chapter Four:
Black Power

You Are Not Alone

Debbie Augenthaler

Chapter Four:
Please Come Back

STORYlab6

PUT to the TEST

create**YOUR**story

STORYlab6

Writing Warm-Ups

Two-minute warm-ups prepare you for the longer writing exercises.

Set a timer for one-minute.

Use the first sentence as a starter sentence, then write for another minute using the second sentence.

Repeat.

WRITING WARM-UP 1

I didn't know who I could trust.
[write for one minute]

I went straight to the bar.
[write for another minute]

WRITING WARM-UP 2

Nothing was familiar.
[write for one minute]

I didn't know the rules.
[write for another minute]

PUT to the **TEST**

Pre-Writing Exploration
Contrast Your Worlds

Pre-Writing Instructions:
Complete each of these three exercises, writing for two minutes on each.

1 YOUR ORDINARY WORLD

Make a list of the details of your Ordinary World.
[write for 2 minutes]

2 YOUR NEW WORLD

Make a second list of the details of your New World.
[write for 2 minutes]

3 CONTRASTING WORLDS

Pair those things from your Ordinary World with those that have the most contrast to your Special World.
[write for 2 minutes]

STORYlab6

Create Your Story

Writing Instructions:

Choose the writing prompt that inspires you. Later, you can explore each prompt.

Write for thirteen minutes without stopping, or overthinking your content. Set your timer!

1 How Information Unfolded

Write about how you gathered information once you entered your new world, the way it unfolded to you.
[write for 13 minutes]

2 How Misfit Functions

Write about feeling like a misfit in your new world how you had to adjust to function inside of it.
[write for 13 minutes]

3 Longing For the Old World

Write about something that happened in your new world that made you long for your old world.
[write for 13 minutes]

4 Compare Your Two Worlds

Compare your two worlds using details of your "Contrast Your Worlds" pre-writing exercise.
[write for 13 minutes]

Who Can Be Trusted?
Allies and Enemies

Is the Hero a good judge of character? One of the tests is learning who can be trusted and relied upon for special services, and who is not be trusted. To make the journey work, the Hero has to become a good judge of character.

Most likely you will find new friends in your new world to help you navigate.

Trust
Thomas R. Smith

It's like so many other things in life
to which you must say no or yes.
So you take your car to the new mechanic.
Sometimes the best thing to do is trust.

The package left with the disreputable-looking
clerk, the check gulped by the night deposit,
the envelope passed by dozens of strangers—
all show up at their intended destinations.

The theft that could have happened doesn't.
Wind finally gets where it was going
through the snowy trees, and the river, even
when frozen, arrives at the right place.

And sometimes you sense how faithfully your life
is delivered, even though you can't read the address.

Reprinted from **Waking Before Dawn**, *Red Dragonfly Press, 2007.*
©2007 Thomas R. Smith. Used with his permission.

STORYlab6

Create Your Story
Writing Instructions:

Choose the writing prompt that inspires you. Later, you can explore each prompt.

Write for thirteen minutes without stopping, or overthinking your content. Set your timer!

1 ENEMY OR ALLY

Write about someone you met in your New World who you didn't know whether they were an ally or an enemy.
[write for 13 minutes]

2 PART OF A TRIBE

Write about being included in a group where you immediately felt you were part of a tribe.
[write for 13 minutes]

3 NEW SIDE OF YOURSELF

Write about a new side of yourself that emerged in the new world and how you had to get to know yourself all over again.
[write for 13 minutes]

*Rock bottom became the solid foundation
on which I rebuilt my life.*

J.K. Rowling

STORYlab7

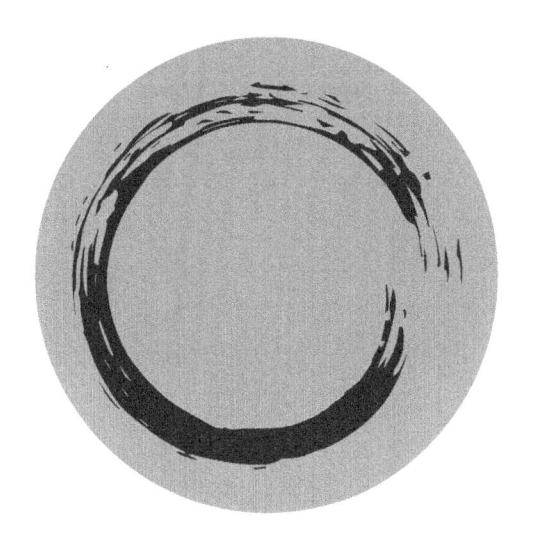

ROCK BOTTOM

Only through death can the Hero be reborn

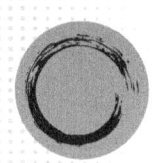

"Sometimes even to live is an act of courage."

Seneca

*"The darker the night, the brighter the stars,
The deeper the grief, the closer is God!"*

Fyodor Dostoyevsky

"We'll never survive! Nonsense. You're only saying that because no one ever has."

William Goldman — The Princess Bride

"Temper us in fire, and we grow stronger. When we suffer, we survive."

Cassandra Clare — City of Heavenly Fire

"Into the darkness they go, the wise and the lovely. "

Edna St. Vincent Millay

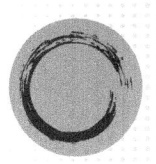

The Crisis of Rock Bottom

This point of a journey is often called the "Dark Night of the Soul." There is a central crisis and this usually occurs near the middle of the book. This is an essential stage of any journey and not a section to be overlooked. The central life-or-death crisis, during which she faces her greatest fear, confronts this most difficult challenge, and she experiences a complete "death." Her whole Journey at this point in the story is now teetering on the edge of failure. It's a breaking apart, a moment the Hero comes close to physically dying, it could also be a moment where failure is imminent. In Sharon Olds' book, it occurs exactly halfway through her book on page 41, in the season of spring after her husband has gone, with the poem *Once in a while I gave up*.

In Lidia Yuknavitch's book, she opens with her dark night, putting it in the very beginning — giving birth to her stillborn daughter. After opening with that scene, she takes us back in time and eventually, halfway through her book, there is a scene of her and her husband throwing their daughter's ashes into the cold river.

Only through "death" and by hitting "rock bottom" can the Hero be reborn, experiencing a resurrection that grants greater powers or insight to see the Journey to the end.

The Hero may directly come in contact with death, or witness the death of a good friend, an earth angel or a mentor. Even worse, the Hero may be responsible for someone's death.

At the stage when the Hero walks away still alive, they feel shocked and also high on surviving, or picking themselves up from *Rock Bottom* and continuing.

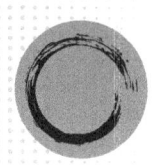

Summary: Rock Bottom — The Crisis

- *Rock Bottom* is the main event of a story.

- *Rock Bottom* can be an illness, where a patient gets worse before he recovers.

- Generally this comes near the middle of a story – every story needs a crisis moment that conveys The Ordeal's sense of death and revival.

- Sometimes it's arriving at the most secret place in your own soul.

- Often referred to as "the dark night of the soul."

- The word crisis comes from a Greek word that means "to separate." A crisis is an event that separates the two halves of the story.

- After crossing this zone, the Hero is metaphorically reborn and nothing will ever be the same.

- This can be defined as the moment when the Hero faces his greatest fear.

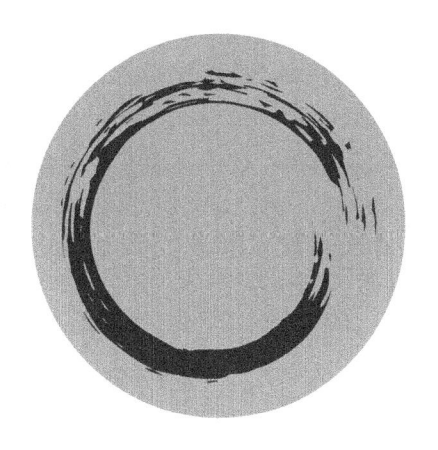

ROCK BOTTOM

LITERARY examples

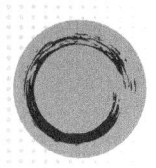

Any Common Desolation
Ellen Bass

can be enough to make you look up
at the yellowed leaves of the apple tree, the few
that survived the rains and frost, shot
with late afternoon sun. They glow a deep
orange-gold against a blue so sheer, a single bird
would rip it like silk. You may have to break
your heart, but it isn't nothing
to know even one moment alive. The sound
of an oar in an oarlock or a ruminant
animal tearing grass. The smell of grated ginger.
The ruby neon of the liquor store sign.
Warm socks. You remember your mother,
her precision a ceremony, as she gathered
the white cotton, slipped it over your toes,
drew up the heel, turned the cuff. A breath
can uncoil as you walk across your own muddy yard,
the big dipper pouring night down over you, and everything
you dread, all you can't bear, dissolves
and, like a needle slipped into your vein—
that sudden rush of the world.

Ellen Bass, "Any Common Desolation" from Indigo. Originally published in Poem-a-Day (November 18, 2016). Copyright © 2016, 2020 by Ellen Bass. Reprinted with the permission of the author and The Permissions Company, LLC on behalf of Copper Canyon Press, coppercanyonpress.org

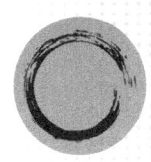

My Darkest Night
Laura Lentz

God—please, I begged.

I had not prayed since I wore out the knees on my monkey pajamas asking for my grandmother to get well again.

I was crying and pacing the faux hardwood floor of my Los Angeles rental. I was up until 4 a.m. researching my medical condition and getting up at 8 a.m. to drive my daughter to school.

I was joining and leaving support groups in the same twenty minutes when I realized *everyone in them was dying.* Maybe I didn't really have the rare cancer, and maybe I did. I had a hard time believing pathology reports because it came on simple white paper with black ink instead of with a symphony and a conductor quieting the string section.

Still, I didn't feel well then. I was falling asleep at my desk at work and no longer fought with my daughter over doing her homework on time. I was tired all the time, and the world had a gray ashen color over it.

I called my friend Mary Ellen and told her I was bargaining with God, Allah, Buddha, The Universe—even the woman at the bank who gave me my balance. *Please,* I seemed to say to her without words, *I might be dying. Make the money last.*

I took my daughter out of school and to New York to see every Broadway play that was appropriate for an eleven year-old *(Wicked, The Lion King)*, and some that weren't appropriate *(Rent).*

And while I was showing my daughter Vincent van Gogh's *Starry Night* at MOMA, I walked deep into my personal dark night and kept praying and bargaining, dragging my too heavy ass onto my treadmill.

Praying to the workout Gods - *give me the energy for one more mile. One more yoga pose.*

The doctor said two to five years and reminded me they wouldn't necessarily be good years. I wouldn't just die when I ran out of time. The organs would *start shutting down,* he said, staring at his scuffed black shoes.

Specialists all over the country confirmed this news.

One day, my friend Mary Ellen told me not to ask The Universe for a mile or a minute, but to ask to stay alive until my daughter didn't need me anymore.

STORYlab7

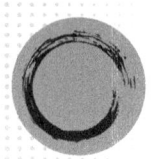

Just ask for that, she said.

A simple prayer.

Many years have passed since that prayer. My daughter is grown and has children and recently she called me and said, *we really need you to watch the kids every Friday.*

I'm here to tell you that nobody can tell you when you are going to die—and prayer does help, even if you are praying to the deepest part of yourself to wake her up and call in her warriors for backup.

No research on prayer or meditation or song or movement could tell me more than I already knew. I watched Tina Turner close her eyes and offer a Buddhist chant and listened to The Lord's Prayer in seven languages.

Mother Theresa said, *May God break my heart so completely that the whole world falls in.*

Our darkest nights always have a way of leading us home.

ROCK BOTTOM

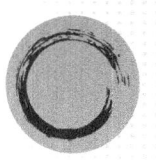

READ

The three examples I offer here are extraordinary moments of hitting an abyss.
Two examples show up in the middle of the books – but Lidia Yuknavitch opens her book with a *Rock Bottom* moment, and it works beautifully, reminding writers that a Hero's journey – can be told out of order. — especially in literature

The Beggar King and the Secret of Happiness

Joel ben Izzy

Page 121—123

You Are Not Alone

Debbie Augenthaler

Page 87—94

The Chronology of Water

Lidia Yuknavitch

Page 29—32

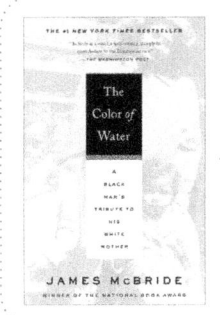

The Color of Water

James McBride

Chapter Fifteen

STORYlab7

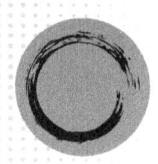

Writing is finding the courage to discover and embrace our truth, and then become the master of that truth.

Laura Lentz

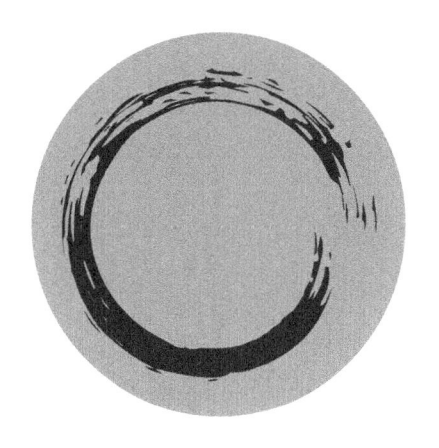

ROCK BOTTOM

create**YOUR**story

STORYlab7

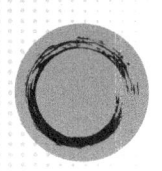

Writing Warm-Ups

Two-minute warm-ups prepare you for the longer writing exercises.

Set a timer for one-minute.

Use the first sentence as a starter sentence, then write for another minute using the second sentence.

Repeat.

WRITING WARM-UP 1

I demand to speak with God.
[write for one minute]

I cannot die, because I have not lived.
[write for another minute]

WRITING WARM-UP 2

I cannot forget my old self.
[write for one minute]

This is the song of Autumn.
[write for another minute]

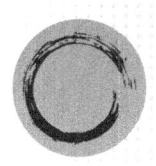

Pre-Writing Inspiration
Sentence Wall

The following is an inspirational sentence wall. Choose a sentence or sentences that resonates for you and write the sentences at the top of your page. When writing your longer writes, use one of these sentences as a Starter Sentence, or wherever it fits into your story.

Because of death, I had to sell everything.

She had gone to feed the roots of the gathering spring.

Afterward comes a lull.

I kept walking slowly into death.

Time slept and I slept.

They say the veils are thin, but I know the veil is gone.

I was the beam of a lightless star.

I'm bowing but not knowing to what.

I walked empty roads and drank shadows.

Remembering the amber taste of honey, I shall not forget you.

Now is the time for the acorn to fall from the tree.

Pre-Writing Exploration

A Part of You Died

Make a list of all the times in your life when you felt a part of you die a little.
[write for 2 minutes]

STORYlab7

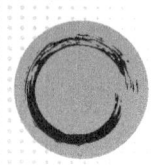

Create Your Story
Writing Instructions:

Choose the writing prompt that inspires you. Later, you can explore each prompt.

Write for thirteen minutes without stopping, or overthinking your content. Set your timer!

1 FACING YOUR GREATEST FEAR

Tell us how you faced death by facing your greatest fear.
[write for 13 minutes]

2 A PART OF YOU DIED

Write about one of the pivotal moments in life when a part of you died.
[write for 13 minutes]

3 GIVING IN

Write about giving in — surrendering to the journey after an ordeal; a moment when you stopped fighting.
[write for 13 minutes]

4 CHEATING DEATH

Write about cheating death – something you survived when so many others failed.
[write for 13 minutes]

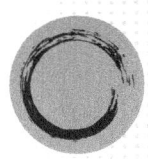

READ

The Beggar King and the Secret of Happiness

Joel ben Izzy

Page 168–170

My Mother upon Hearing News of Her Mother's Death

Cathy Linh Che

She opened her mouth and a moose came out, a donkey, and an ox—out of her mouth, years of animal grief. I lead her to the bed. She held my hand and followed. She said, Chết rồi, and like that, the cord was cut, the thread snapped, and the cable that tied my mother to her mother broke. And now her eyes red as a market fish. And now, she dropped like laundry on the bed.

The furniture moved toward her, the kitchen knives and spoons, the vibrating spoons—they dragged the tablecloth, the corner tilting in, her mouth a sinkhole. She wanted all of it: the house and the car too, and the flowers she planted, narcissus and hoa mai, which cracked open each spring—the sky, she brought it low until the air was hot and wet and broke into a rain—

the torrents like iron ropes you could climb up, only I couldn't. I was drowning in it. I was swirled in. I leapt into her mouth, her throat, her gut, and stayed inside with the remnants of my former life. I ate the food she ate and drank the milk she drank. I grew until I crowded the furnishings. I edged out her organs, her swollen heart. I grew up and out so large that I became a woman, wearing my mother's skin.

Copyright © 2014 by Cathy Linh Che. Reprinted by permission of the author

STORYlab7

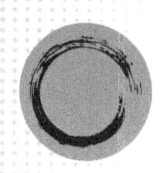

Create Your Story
Writing Instructions:

Choose the writing prompt that inspires you. Later, you can explore each prompt.

Write for thirteen minutes without stopping, or overthinking your content. Set your timer!

1 DEATH AND CHANGE

Write the way you were changed by someone's death: Perhaps the death of a mentor in your story, a parent or other family member.
[write for 13 minutes]

2 FOREVER ALTERED

Write about how the story of someone's death you never met, altered you.
[write for 13 minutes]

3 LAST WORDS

Write about a conversation you had with someone when they were preparing to die or right before they died..
[write for 13 minutes]

*"They can award me with the greatest accolades and reward me with the finest diamonds.
They can name days and streets after me, canonize and celebrate me.
They can make me the queen of their kingdom, the president of their nation.
They can carry my picture in their wallets and whisper my name in their prayers
but, tell me, what is all this worth
if your voice isn't the one calling me home?"*

Kamand Kojouri

STORYlab8

CELEBRATIONS

Surviving is a blessing (and a curse)

"You need to spend time crawling alone through shadows to truly appreciate what it is to stand in the sun."
Shaun Hick

"The reward is in the risk."
Rachel Cohn — Dash & Lily's Book of Dares

"Love is the soul's reward for all the previous heartbreaks..."
Virginia Alison

"The thing about changing the world... Once you do it, the world's all different."
Joss Whedon — Buffy the Vampire Slayer: The Long Way Home

CELEBRATIONS

The Honor of Surviving

We've all heard of the Phoenix rising out of the ashes – in this part of the STORYquest, the Hero has survived his ordeal — his near death experience and the metaphorical dragon is no longer there. It's time to celebrate, to claim or receive accolades and honors for making it this far. In this part of the story the Hero recognizes he has changed. This experience separates him from most of the world. It's a kind of deserved rebirth because his old self has died and he is shedding his old skin with the knowledge that his world is forever changed, and so has he. There is no turning back now because the Hero isn't the same person. There is no turning back because the Hero no longer sees the world through the same lens and so no place will ever look the same. The past and the *World of Before* will now be seen through a wise lens, with the wisdom and compassion of a survivor.

What does he bring with him into this new awakening? The Hero has empathy and compassion and a deep reverence for those who did not survive, who did not come this far. This is where the Hero receives praise and honors - a "purple heart" for surviving. Now, the windows are open and the storm is over and children are out playing in the rain. Now, as poet Lisel Mueller writes in her poem, *Small Poem about the Hounds and the Hares*, "the hounds, drunk on the blood of the hares, begin to talk of how soft were their pelts, how graceful their leaps, how lovely their scared, gentle eyes."

There may be a feast, there may be a celebration in this part of your STORYquest. The Hero has little energy left, and this is a time of refueling and regrouping. Strength is now needed and rest is in order. This is another critical part of your Hero's journey, and one that cannot be overlooked. In this section of your story, the writer needs to allow the reader to exhale. In the previous chapter the reader may have been holding their breath, waiting to see the outcome. Now the reader can relax, they have the space to continue with the story. The wild ride has paused (for now).

This is a critical part of your book to make an emotional connection with your reader and allow them to rise in strength with you.

In Debbie Augenthaler's book, *You Are Not Alone*, she has survived a year without her husband, has moved to a new place in the city and gathers with her clan in Tulsa Oklahoma – they drink and celebrate and the celebration turns into a sacred ceremony. In Lidia Yuknavitch's *Chronology of Water*, it's her first meeting with Andy Mingo after her DUI and community service and in Joel Ben Izzy's *Beggar King and the Secret of Happiness*, it's after hearing a story from his mentor and coming to the realization how close he came to dying. He sits in the middle of the family living room in the early morning hours waving a blank flag.

The Treasure

The Hero may take possession of something – a house, an apartment, a bank account, a piece of jewelry or a Tarot card deck. There is symbology at this point in the Hero's Journey and sometimes it's in the form of a magic elixir – maybe even an unusual cure for cancer. Many times it's peace of mind or happiness.

Initiation

If the Hero has cheated death, survived deep grief, won a battle, he has gone through an initiation. He is now in a new group of survivors. He may be the holder of a secret that even if he spoke it, others not part of his tribe might not understand it. He may be given a new name to identify with his new self.

Super Powers

At this point in the Quest, the Hero may recognize superpowers emerging from his experience. It's as if he has been looking through a fog and the fog has lifted and he sees clearly the past, the present and the future as if they are one. Now he is awake, and this means he can stand in the universal question, understand the strange patterns in life. He may have extra sensory perceptions now or an ability to dream the future. He may be seeing himself in the mirror for the very first time. This is a very clarifying and magical part of the story.

Summary: Celebration

- The Hero has paused to recalibrate.

- This scene allows the reader to rest also, and breathe easy.

- The Hero has sacrificed, and now he must have his reward.

- The Hero comes out of this with Super Powers.

- The Hero has empathy and compassion, because he has suffered.

- Always there is a deeper knowing, having been through the darkness.

CELEBRATIONS

LITERARYexamples

STORYlab8

READ

The following three scenes are classic Hero's Journey scenes after an ordeal.

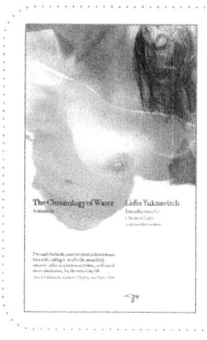

The Chronology of Water

Lidia Yuknavitch

Page 233, Conversion

You Are Not Alone

Debbie Augenthaler

Chapter 12
The Butterfly Clan

The Beggar King and the Secret of Happiness

Joel ben Izzy

Page 134-136

The Color of Water

James McBride

Page 274 - 278

CELEBRATIONS

createYOURstory

STORYlab8

Writing Warm-Ups

Two-minute warm-ups prepare you for the longer writing exercises.

Set a timer for one-minute.

Use the first sentence as a starter sentence, then write for another minute using the second sentence.

Repeat.

WRITING WARM-UP 1

Now it seems I will always have too much of everything I love.
[write for one minute]

I put down my sword.
[write for another minute]

WRITING WARM-UP 2

I drank the elixir and it was bitter.
[write for one minute]

We feasted and drank until dawn.
[write for another minute]

Pre-Writing Inspiration
Sentence Wall

> **BEFORE YOU WRITE**
>
> *Choose a sentence from this sentence wall to use as a starter sentence, or somewhere in your chapter.*
>
> We'll drown the hour with song.
>
> Victory marches with bugles down a street.
>
> The party goes on forever.
>
> To know the soul exceeds its confinement.
>
> Victory was scotch and anecdotes.
>
> Lie in the arms of a night long fire.
>
> We stand at last, where the white gleam of our bright star is cast.
>
> To reimagine my life.
>
> My one hand holding tight my other hand.
>
> We've broken laws, both written and unwritten.
>
> This is the body of light.
>
> This story will change with each telling.

STORYlab8

Create Your Story
Writing Instructions:

Choose the writing prompt that inspires you. Later, you can explore each prompt.

Write for thirteen minutes without stopping, or overthinking your content. Set your timer!

---

1 STORY OF SURVIVAL

Show us a time after an ordeal, when your adrenalin was high and you gathered with others to tell the story of survival.
[write for 13 minutes]

2 MIRROR IMAGE

Write about seeing yourself differently in the mirror, because you have changed..
[write for 13 minutes]

3 UNEXPECTED LOVE STORY

Write about unexpected love that showed up after. Show us a scene with a lover, a friend, a child or a parent.
[write for 13 minutes]

After the Disaster
Abigail Deutsch

New York City, 2001

One night, not long after the disaster,
as our train was passing Astor,
the car door opened with a shudder
and a girl came flying down the aisle,
hair that looked to be all feathers
and a half-moon smile
making open air of our small car.
The crowd ignored her or they muttered
"Hey, excuse me" as they passed her
when the train had paused at Rector.
The specter crowed "Excuse me," swiftly
turned, and ran back up the corridor,
then stopped for me.
We dove under the river.
She took my head between her fingers,
squeezing till the birds began to stir.
And then from out my eyes and ears
a flock came forth — I couldn't think or hear
or breathe or see within that feather-world
so silently I thanked her.
Such things were common after the disaster.

First appeared in Poetry, *used by permission of the author.*

STORYlab8

Create Your Story
Writing Instructions:

Choose the writing prompt that inspires you. Later, you can explore each prompt.

Write for thirteen minutes without stopping, or overthinking your content. Set your timer!

1 ENTER THE MAGIC

Describe the magic that entered your world once the event was over.
[write for 13 minutes]

2 YOUR PERSONAL EPIPHANY

Tell us about something you knew for sure that you hadn't known before the ordeal —your personal epiphany.
[write for 13 minutes]

3 YOU PUT YOUR SWORD DOWN

Describe the mythological sword you put down when the battle was over.
[write for 13 minutes]

The greater difficulty, the more glory in surmounting it. Skillful pilots gain their reputation from storms and tempests.

Epicurus

STORYlab9

TROUBLE AGAIN

The long road back

STORYlab9

"Difficulties show men what they are. In case of any difficulty, God has pitted you against a rough antagonist that you may be a conqueror, and this cannot be without toil."

Epictetus

"It was an interesting dilemma and with all such dilemmas an opportunity might emerge. 'How best to turn this setback into an advantage.'"

Raymond E. Feist

"Setbacks allow us to take a step back and look at the view from a whole."

Brittany Burgunder

"Are you worthy of realizing your dream? If you said yes, there is no short cut. You're going to encounter setback after setback until you realize your dream."

Assegid Habtewold

"When surrounded by the ashes of all that I once cherished, despite my best efforts I can find no room to be thankful. But standing there amidst endless ash I must remember that although the ashes surround me, God surrounds the ashes. And once that realization settles upon me, I am what I thought I could never be ... I am thankful for ashes."

Craig D. Lounsbrough

"I ask you to judge me by the enemies I have made."

Franklin D. Roosevelt

TROUBLE AGAIN

The Quest Continues
The Long Road Back

The Hero has rested. She has celebrated. She has learned her lessons. She doesn't expect most people will believe what she's been through and now she has a choice. Stay in the new world or return to the *World of Before* to tell others about it and share the knowledge. Whether the Hero creates a whole new world for herself or returns to the *World of Before*, the Hero is again at a turning point. This begins Act Three of the journey, when the she rededicates herself to the quest. Even though the Hero has fulfilled a dream, something may be amiss. Her life might not match the Quest, or she may have a strange feeling something might go wrong again.

There might be a turn in the story — another crisis that sets the Hero on a new and final road of trials before the story is over. It's a temporary setback, but this scene is an important part of the Hero's Quest. Most Heroes return to the place where the journey began, but many continue to a totally new destination.

As a writer, we need to think of *Trouble Again* as an uphill climb after the downward fall. The Hero is much healthier and stronger, she will have trouble ahead, or perhaps an enemy chasing on her heels. All of this serves as a reminder of why she started her quest at all, and what wisdoms she learned along the way.

In Lidia Yuknavitch's book *The Chronology of Water*, she meets Mingo, a student at the university where she is teaching. Shortly after meeting him, she gets fired from her job for having an affair with a student. Lidia's last trial is when the staff at the university used shame before firing her.

In Debbie Augenthaler's book, *You Are Not Alone*, Debbie enters the dating world again, only to have a horrible date arranged by a friend where everything goes wrong, forcing Debbie to again face her life without her husband, reopenng her wound.

In Joel Ben Izzy's book, *The Beggar King and the Secret of Happiness*, he has to face the death of a parent, one final setback before he returns to his *World of Before*.

If we look at the Quest as a solar eclipse, the moon is blocking the light of the sun. Now the light is returning slowly. The Hero is able to see with a new lens.

It's time to climb back into the light.

STORYlab9

Summary: Trouble Again, The Long Road Back

- This is a time of implementing the lessons learned from the Quest.

- The wisdom and magic dissolves into the everyday, making the Hero question if the magic really happened.

- Others will question Hero's story. This is the part of the story where he reminds himself how important it is to refocus.

- The enemy may reappear for one final challenge and the Hero has *Trouble Again*.

- Even though the he has one more challenge to overcome, he now has all the wisdom to meet that challenge.

TROUBLE AGAIN

LITERARY examples

Relax
Ellen Bass

Bad things are going to happen.
Your tomatoes will grow a fungus
and your cat will get run over.
Someone will leave the bag with the ice cream
melting in the car and throw
your blue cashmere sweater in the drier.
Your husband will sleep
with a girl your daughter's age, her breasts spilling
out of her blouse. Or your wife
will remember she's a lesbian
and leave you for the woman next door. The other cat—
the one you never really liked—will contract a disease
that requires you to pry open its feverish mouth
every four hours. Your parents will die.
No matter how many vitamins you take,
how much Pilates, you'll lose your keys,
your hair and your memory. If your daughter
doesn't plug her heart
into every live socket she passes,
you'll come home to find your son has emptied
the refrigerator, dragged it to the curb,
and called the used appliance store for a pick up—drug money.
There's a Buddhist story of a woman chased by a tiger.
When she comes to a cliff, she sees a sturdy vine
and climbs half way down. But there's also a tiger below.
And two mice—one white, one black—scurry out
and begin to gnaw at the vine. At this point
she notices a wild strawberry growing from a crevice.
She looks up, down, at the mice.
Then she eats the strawberry.
So here's the view, the breeze, the pulse
in your throat. Your wallet will be stolen, you'll get fat,
slip on the bathroom tiles of a foreign hotel
and crack your hip. You'll be lonely.
Oh taste how sweet and tart
the red juice is, how the tiny seeds
crunch between your teeth.

Ellen Bass, "Relax" from Like a Beggar. Copyright © 2014 by Ellen Bass. Reprinted with the permission of the author and The Permissions Company, LLC on behalf of Copper Canyon Press, coppercanyonpress.org.

TROUBLE AGAIN

READ

The following four scenes are classic Hero's Journey scenes after an ordeal.

The Beggar King and the Secret of Happiness

Joel ben Izzy

Page 134-136

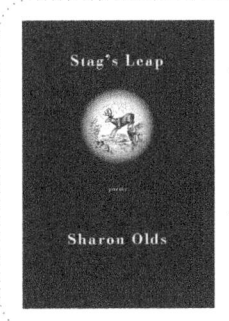

Stag's Leap

Sharon Olds

Approaching Godthab
page 39

You Are Not Alone

Debbie Augenthaler

Chapter 13
Ready for Dating

The Chronology of Water

Lidia Yuknavitch

Page 233, Conversion

137

The Middle
Cheryl Sterner

I'm a tour guide for Destruction.
I've built and blown up a hundred cities searching for you,
lost and found over the course of many lifetimes.

If things are cushy and cute,
pristine and perfectly placed,
you'll never know God or her legion.

I prefer a Hammer,
Dynamite,
C4
to lay waste to the foundations of all I've built.

If you want to know the Greatest Secret,
you need to study explosives.

When the bombs begin to dissipate and the rubble stills,
I sit in the middle and cry.
Desolation needs to be baptized.

It's not in the crumbling itself, though this, too, is precious -
but in the stillness that follows.
The ripping wound of all that has been torn
from your clutched breast.

In the Last Breath of something loved
God whispers.

TROUBLE AGAIN

createYOURstory

STORYlab9

Writing Warm-Ups

Two-minute warm-ups prepare you for the longer writing exercises.

Set a timer for one-minute.

Use the first sentence as a starter sentence, then write for another minute using the second sentence.

Repeat.

WRITING WARM-UP 1

I have nine lives.
[write for one minute]

I had one more hurdle, but this time I was ready.
[write for another minute]

WRITING WARM-UP 2

Trouble came for one last performance.
[write for one minute]

Tell everyone I am coming home.
[write for another minute]

TROUBLE AGAIN

Pre-Writing Inspiration
Sentence Wall

> **BEFORE YOU WRITE**
>
> *Choose a sentence from this sentence wall to use as a starter sentence, or somewhere in your chapter.*
>
> Forgiven, they go free of you, and you of them.
>
> The enemy was a dark angel.
>
> I will not give the mosquito her share.
>
> The sun is the enemy of poets and lovers.
>
> The enemies have delivered themselves to destruction.
>
> The first time, I slept with the enemy. The second time...
>
> The worst friend and enemy is but death.

STORYlab9

Create Your Story
Writing Instructions:

Choose the writing prompt that inspires you. Later, you can explore each prompt.

Write for thirteen minutes without stopping, or overthinking your content. Set your timer!

1 LAST SETBACK

Write about a last setback you had, and how you coped with it this time.
[write for 13 minutes]

2 SURPRISED BY THE ENEMY

Write about how you thought the enemy was gone, and how they surprised you again.
[write for 13 minutes]

3 RETALIATION

Write about a time someone retaliated against the New You.
[write for 13 minutes]

4 UNCERTAINTY

Write about a time you were leaving one world, and not certain of your destination.
[write for 13 minutes]

Magical Flight & Sacrifice

In his book *The Writer's Journey*, Christopher Vogler mentions there is often a whimsical transformation of objects and a magical flight that takes place in fairytales. Joseph Campbell also mentioned Magical Flights as a repeated theme in mythology suggesting the Hero's attempts to get away from the enemy and flee from their power. This is a wonderful opportunity to invite magic into your story.

What the Hero drops into the path of the enemy to distract them will sometimes represent a last major sacrifice. Lidia Yuknavtich sacrificed her job for something much more profound. Sharon Olds must let go of the old husband to embrace her new reality, using flight and the metaphor of the silver kite.

Annunciation
C. Dale Young

I learned to hide my wings almost immediately,
learned to tuck and bandage them down.
Long before the accident, before the glass shattering
and that scene going dim, dimmer, and then dark,
before the three fractures at the axis, three cracks

in the bone, it had already begun. My voice
had begun to deepen, the sound of it
suddenly more my father's than my own. My beard
had started growing, my bones growing, my bones
sore from the speed of their growth, and there,

at fourteen years of age, the first tugging
of the muscles between my shoulder blades.
It began as a tiny ache. It was just a minor irritation.
Day after day passed, and this ache grew,
and then the tips of the cartilaginous wings

began to tent my skin. Father Callahan
had already warned that in each of us
there was both potential for bad and good.
When trying to shave for the first time, I nicked
my cheek, the bleeding slow but continuous.

STORYlab9

Standing there, dabbing at this small cut with tissue paper,
the first tear surprised me, the left wing heaving through
that fleshy mound of muscle between my shoulder blades
and then the skin. I buckled and, on my knees, the right wing
presented itself more rapidly than the left.

When I stood, there in the mirror, my wings outstretched
with their tiny feathers wet, almost glutinous, a quick
ribbon of blood snaking down my back. You wonder
why I am such a master of avoidance, such a master
of what is withheld. Is there any wonder, now?

I had no idea then they would wither and fall off
in a few weeks. When Father Callahan patted
my head in the sacristy and told me I was
a good boy, a really good boy, an extraordinary boy,
I wanted to be anything but extraordinary.

Annunciation from **The Halo** *©2016 by C. Dale Young.*
Reprinted with permission of Four Way Books. All rights reserved.

TROUBLE AGAIN

Write Your Story
Writing Instructions:

Choose one of these writing prompts or do all three.

Set your timer and write for thirteen minutes without stopping, or overthinking your content.

1 FANTASTICAL TRUTH

Write a time of after when you began to doubt the truth of your own story because it was so fantastical.
[write for 13 minutes]

2 FLYING FOR PERSPECTIVE

Tell us about flying and looking down on the journey beneath you—your mythological and metaphorical wings that took you on the last leg of your journey.
[write for 13 minutes]

3 FINAL SACRIFICE

Write about leaving behind something of value as a sacrifice, as you decide what is really important.
[write for 13 minutes]

The Thing Is
Ellen Bass

to love life, to love it even
when you have no stomach for it
and everything you've held dear
crumbles like burnt paper in your hands,
your throat filled with the silt of it.
When grief sits with you, its tropical heat
thickening the air, heavy as water
more fit for gills than lungs;
when grief weights you like your own flesh
only more of it, an obesity of grief,
you think, How can a body withstand this?
Then you hold life like a face
between your palms, a plain face,
no charming smile, no violet eyes,
and you say, yes, I will take you
I will love you, again.

from Mules of Love (BOA Editions, ©2002)

STORYlab10

REBIRTH

The climax of your story

147

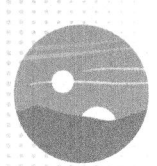

"I can't tell whether a revived man would appreciate his second chance or yearn for the stolen serenity."

Ahmed Mostafa

"Writing is an act of resurrection."

Laura Lentz

"A bridge of silver wings stretches from the dead ashes of an unforgiving nightmare to the jeweled vision of a life started anew."

Aberjhani

"Only after disaster can we be resurrected."

Chuck Palahniuk, Fight Club

"It is not more surprising to be born twice than once; everything in nature is resurrection."

Voltaire

"It is such a letdown to rise from the dead and have your friends not recognize you."

Rob Bell

REBIRTH

Finally, The Climax of Your Story

This critical part of your story is where the Hero gets to live again. As a writer, it's time to show us the change in you or your character – not tell us about it. You show us by the character's behavior, their appearance.

In Sharon Olds books *Stag's Leap*, she shows us how her whole perception has been altered in Poem of *Thanks* and *Left-Wife Bop*. The books entertain a new perspective after her final sacrifice, when she and her husband part equals.

Lidia Yuknavitch writes "It is possible to carry life and death in the same sentence. In the same body. It is possible to carry love and pain. In the water, this body I have come to slides through the wet with a history. What if there is hope in that." Her climax comes when the paramedics take her husband away in the middle of the night — and even a little later in the story, when she and her sister scatter their father's ashes.

Maybe the Climax is Physical, Maybe It is Emotional

This part of the story is a reminder of death that is always in our shadows, beckoning us, and it's a final test. The Universe is serious now. She wants to know if you will fail, if you will take the bait and make a mistake in judgment, risking everything.

In Joel ben Izzy's book, The *Beggar King and the Secret of Happiness*, Joel's final crisis is physical and risky. He decides to have an operation to possibly restore his voice. During the surgery, where he must be awake for the procedure, we are taken through the climax with the Hero. It's a harrowing scene, where Joel must face his final life altering challenge.

The Climax Can Be A Whisper

We all think of climaxes as showdowns or big events, and they can be — but sometimes they are a quiet whisper, a final understanding — a gentle, rolling wave finally headed home to the shoreline, one you can barely see. For some grief stories, it's a moment of relief in the acceptance of the fate, where our entanglements with grief are at last released.

The Climax Can Be Earth Shattering

Often a climax is a threat to the entire world, not just the Hero. In Debbie Augenthaler's book, *You Are Not Alone*, a friend calls and tells her to look at the television. It's September 11, 2001, and the weeks that follow are challenging. This earth-shattering historical climax unites so many in a shared loss, and the final ordeal shows Debbie how the seeds of her own sorrow have been planted to help others. Many people come to Debbie because she understands sudden loss.

Emotional Relief

This part of the book should be a final emotional release for the reader. It could also feed the reader with a series of lessons and breakthroughs. In this part of the book, it's all about a raised consciousness – both for the Hero and the reader. If someone dies in a book, often the death happens here – perhaps a main character dies but in a connective way they are resurrected in the hearts of the Hero and the reader.

Summary: Rebirth

- People change by degrees, not all at once. This part of story is the final degree of change, the final growth spurt of the Hero.

- Some climaxes are like a whisper.

  This is the final moment where the character steps fully into his new self
- and we see him changed.

- This is a time of metaphorical death and rebirth.

- This part of the book teaches the reader something — lessons and breakthroughs carry through to the reader for a deeper understanding.

REBIRTH

LITERARY examples

Carnal Knowledge
Constance Frenzen

I was initiated
into carnal knowledge
by a sorceress who seduced me
with her piercing gaze
through my window,
in the silence of the night,
in the light of no moon,
within the shadow
of shining stars.

She whispered me her apprentice
and I followed, deep into dark forests
beneath circles of ancient trees
whose gnarled arms
spread beds of dead leaves
upon which she had me lay,
performing rituals of intimacy
stewed in juices of mist
beneath the raven's cry.

And I drank from her potions
by the raging sea
where tides lay open wombs of sand
jeweled with clam shells
and starfish and coral.
Where we bathed in the blood of the moon,
as our horses, wild with freedom,
stirred clouds of luminescence
beneath their pounding hooves.

And I followed her on pilgrimages
to mountain plateaus
where wildflowers witnessed
her rites of my disrobing
and the sacraments which followed,
while they reveled
and quivered in the wind.

REBIRTH

She carved the earth into sections,
brewing her sorcery
with the wisdom of Woman,
initiating me to cull my conjuring
from within the elements of my eyes,
the movement of my mouth,
the taunting of my touch—
to embody the feminine potions
of the sacred within the mystery,
in the ways of this world.

©2019 permission by author

STORYlab10

READ

You Are Not Alone

Debbie Augenthaler

Chapter 12
Turning Point

The Beggar King and the Secret of Happiness

Joel ben Izzy

Chapter 13
The Fox in the Garden

The Chronology of Water

Lidia Yuknavitch

Page 263, Angina

Stag's Leap

Sharon Olds

Poem of Thanks, Left-Wife Bop
Pages 82-83

REBIRTH

createYOURstory

STORYlab10

Writing Warm-Ups

Two-minute warm-ups prepare you for the longer writing exercises.

Set a timer for one-minute.

Use the first sentence as a starter sentence, then write for another minute using the second sentence.

Repeat.

WRITING WARM-UP 1

Suffer me one more time.
[write for one minute]

This beauty breaking on my eyes.
[write for another minute]

WRITING WARM-UP 2

Breath spills back.
[write for one minute]

I forgot to be dead.
[write for another minute]

Pre-Writing Inspiration
Sentence Wall

Before You Write

Choose a sentence from this sentence wall to use as a starter sentence, or somewhere in your chapter.

I was raised on love and miracles.

I dissolved in the mirror and then reappeared looking almost the same.

My new voice was tender, but strong.

As if I was standing on my own grave.

The image of my old self was reflected back to me in the eyes of my friends.

The dreamer finally awakens inside the dream.

I carried my own name like a giant shield.

My lifeline seemed to grow another inch.

STORYlab10

Create Your Story
Writing Instructions:

Choose the writing prompt that inspires you. Later, you can explore each prompt.

Write for thirteen minutes without stopping, or overthinking your content. Set your timer!

1 SHOW HOW YOU HAVE CHANGED

Show us how your behavior and appearance has changed so much, perhaps someone you know well almost mistakes you for someone else, or you are shocked to see the changes show up in your own mirror.
[write for 13 minutes]

2 YOUR FINAL ORDEAL

Write about the final ordeal that includes a brush with death, or a final challenge you have to overcome to step into your new self.
[write for 13 minutes]

3 THE EVOLUTION OF YOU

Write about how this death or ordeal is easier to handle and why —show us the person you became by the way you handle this now.
[write for 13 minutes]

REBIRTH

Incorporation

Rebirth is an opportunity for a Hero to show he has taken in every lesson from every character he has met along the way – the mentors, the allies and even the enemies! Incorporation literally means he has made the lessons of the road part of his whole being. An ideal climax would test everything he's learned, and allow him to show that he has absorbed the best of all the lessons in the story.

Create Your Story
Writing Instructions:

Choose the writing prompt that inspires you. Later, you can explore each prompt.

Write for thirteen minutes without stopping, or overthinking your content. Set your timer!

1 A FINAL EXHALE

Write about the time when you felt the weight of your journey fall away—an exhale..
[write for 13 minutes]

2 A MOMENT OF JOY

Describe a moment of joy and relief that let you relax toward a new way of being.
[write for 13 minutes]

*All water has a perfect memory and
is forever trying to get back to where it was.*
Toni Morrison

STORYlab 11

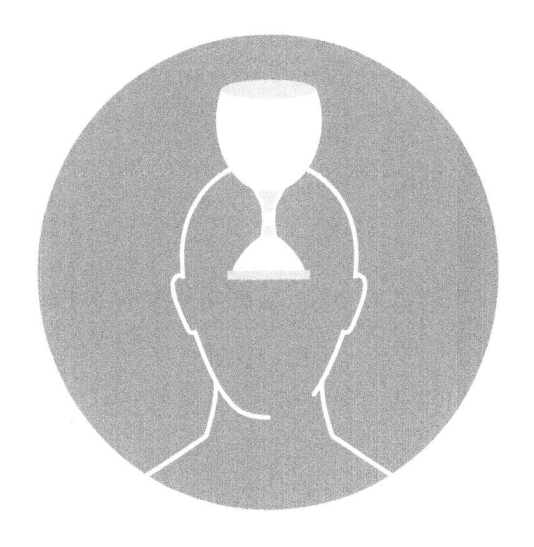

BRINGING the MAGIC HOME

Home is where the story lives

STORYlab11

"The seekers have come home."

Joseph Campbell

"You are your own magical elixir. Waste not one drop."

A.D. Posey

"At the end of the day, it isn't where I came from. Maybe home is somewhere I'm going and never have been before."

Warsan Shire

"Everything is going to be fine in the end. If it's not fine it's not the end."

Oscar Wilde

"Life is such that beginnings and endings are neither. For in fact, they perpetually lay the groundwork for the other."

Craig D. Lounsbrough

BRINGING the MAGIC HOME

You Can Go Home Again

Thomas Wolfe so famously wrote "you can't go home again" and we all know this is not true. Perhaps he meant to write "you can't go home as the same person again." If the Hero returns home everyone looks different because he is forever changed. If he doesn't return to the home he left, the Hero creates a new home – either way he has something to share now that he has completed this journey.

The Hero is forever changed – different because he answered the call, drank from the wisdom, survived trials and then, he fell from grace. If he returns to his starting place, his "Ithaka" (see page xiii) — he brings wisdom to share, or something that can heal a wounded community.

He will come home changed and share his story, knowledge, and new sensibility with his people.

By interacting with the Hero, his people in the old world will begin to change. By healing his own wounds, the Hero begins to heal the wounds of others.

New Questions

It's okay for new questions to come up at the end of the story, but questions raised in the book must be answered now. A fairy-tale ending is not necessary (and often annoying to the reader), but completely "open ended" endings may be too unsatisfying for the reader. Some stories need an open ending, and as I have told my students many times, the ending will almost write itself and show you what is needed.

In Joel ben Izzy's, *The Beggar King and the Secret of Happiness*, his last chapter carries the title of his book, closing the circle. He ends with a fable that begins his book.

In Debbie Augenthaler's book, *You Are Not Alone*, she returns home in a beautiful poem, and home becomes something other than a place with a kitchen and a bed – it becomes the light that connects us all far beyond the death of the body. She becomes the wisdom teller, having survived and transcended her experience; she invites us all to do the same.

In *The Color of Water*, James McBride finally takes his mother home to Suffolk Virginia to face the ghosts of her past. The author, her son, ponders all the reasons his white mother should have stayed on the Jewish side, but shows deep gratitude for her choices.

Summary of Two Ending Story Forms:

Closing the Circle Story Form

- This ending has a sense of closure and completion.

- The ending returns to the beginning.

- Perhaps *Returning with the Magic* is metaphorical, or the writer brings back something from the beginning of the book through a quote, a sentence, a sentiment or dialogue.

- This is the most popular, and helps the audience to see how much the Hero has changed.

- This can be a comforting and reassuring ending to your story, something that will emotionally satisfy the reader.

- This is a great ending if your book begins with a mysterious, unresolved situation — this is the chance for full resolution.

- The writer must be careful to avoid cliché's.

Open-Ended Story Form

- A sense of unanswered questions and unresolved conflicts.

- It's an interesting, but sometimes risky approach.

- It allows the reader to decide what the ending means.

- The "debate" or opening questions in the book continue in the minds and hearts of the audience.

- Some questions have no answers, and some have many answers – you are inviting the reader to stand in the question.

About The Magic

The Magic is the proof of the Hero, something she brings home to show the worlds she visited and the lessons she learned. It can be literal or metaphoric.

It represents three things: change, success and proof of the Quest.

The Magician
Laura Lentz

My father disappeared often –
an accomplished magician,
he showed my mother
how to slice him in half,
push his head, with torso
to one side of the house,
his legs to another
For days he would remain
this way,
in two boxes,
never once asking
to be made whole again,
never once asking for any of us
to push him back together.

We moved around him as though
he wasn't there – set the table,
watched television,
went to school.
Eventually, the red scarf
would turn into a dove,
the wind would rattle the windows

and he would return to us,
in his suit and tie
fresh from the commuter train.

He opened the front door
of our house
with an odd look on his face,
as if seeing us all
for the very first time –

the woman he loved
coming from the kitchen,
his children rushing toward him
in relief,
their small arms wrapping around
his unsturdy legs,
pulling his hands free,
making him whole once again.

©2003 by Laura Lentz.

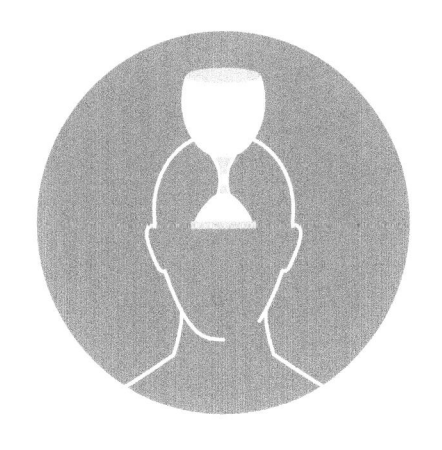

BRINGING the MAGIC HOME

LITERARY examples

STORYlab11

READ

The Chronology of Water

Lidia Yuknavitch

A Small Ocean
Pages 289-294

Stag's Leap

Sharon Olds

What Left?
Page 89

The Beggar King and the Secret of Happiness

Joel ben Izzy

Chapter 14
The Secret of Happiness

You Are Not Alone

Debbie Augenthaler

Welcome Home
Pages 219-223

The Color of Water

James McBride

Finding Ruthie
Pages 259-278

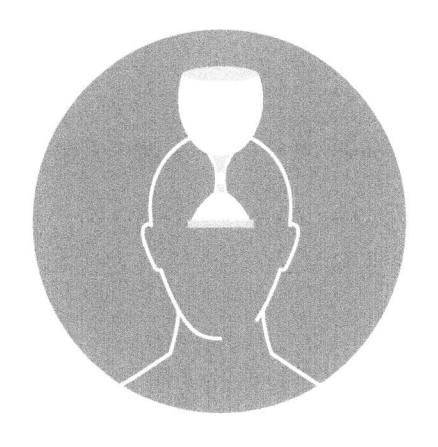

BRINGING the MAGIC HOME

create**YOUR**story

STORYlab11

Writing Warm-Ups

Two-minute warm-ups prepare you for the longer writing exercises.

Set a timer for one-minute.

Use the first sentence as a starter sentence, then write for another minute using the second sentence.

Repeat.

WRITING WARM-UP 1

The end lives inside the beginning.
[write for one minute]

The moon was my witness.
[write for another minute]

WRITING WARM-UP 2

It was worth it.
[write for one minute]

The time came to return home.
[write for another minute]

Pre-Writing Inspiration
Sentence Wall

Before You Write

Choose a sentence from this sentence wall to use as a starter sentence, or somewhere in your chapter.

I ended up where I started.

I wonder if this quiet inside of me is the magic.

We all want to stay in summer forever.

Nobody knows how anything can be like it is.

Time moved backward, piecing together the elements.

The taste of the journey is alive on my tongue.

I released my dreams into the dawn.

My childhood grew up.

And so the beginning was disguised as an end.

Where I ended was where I began.

STORYlab11

Create Your Story
Writing Instructions:

Choose the writing prompt that inspires you. Later, you can explore each prompt.

Write for thirteen minutes without stopping, or overthinking your content. Set your timer!

---

1 ONE BIG MESSAGE

Write something you know for sure that all your life experiences have led you to — a final message that has become the magic you want to share with the world.
[write for 13 minutes]

2 OLD HOME, NEW HOME

Write about what it was like when you returned home, even if home wasn't the place from where your journey began. Perhaps a new world that felt like home..
[write for 13 minutes]

3 SHARING GIFTS

Write about the first time you shared your gifts with another person – someone you helped with your new knowledge from your journey.
[write for 13 minutes]

4 MAGICAL WAKE OF YOU

Write about all the magic that now shows up in the wake of you.
[write for 13 minutes]

Write Two Endings to Your Story

You have known the ending of your story all along, but chances are while creating this book you have been in a place of discovery. Your final discovery is happening now, in the ending. Discover the possibilities by playing with different endings to your story with this final exercise.

Create Your Story
Writing Instructions:

Choose the writing prompt that inspires you. Later, you can explore each prompt.

Write for thirteen minutes without stopping, or overthinking your content. Set your timer!

1 LINGERING QUESTION

Write an ending where there is resolution, but a final question that goes unanswered. What is that question and how is the Hero living with an unanswered question?
[write for 13 minutes]

2 FAIRY TALE ENDING

Write a "Fairy Tale" ending filled with clichés and see what happens to your story —when you are finished highlight the magic you love and consider incorporating it into your story..
[write for 13 minutes]

3 WHAT'S NEXT

Write about the Hero looking out onto the horizon for his next Quest.
[write for 13 minutes]

This is why the work is so important. Its power doesn't lie in the me that lives in the words as much as in the heart's blood pumping behind the eye that is reading, the muscle behind the desire that is sparked by the word – hope as a living state that propels us, open-eyed and fearful, into all the battles of our lives. And some of those battles we do not win.

But some of them we do.

Audre Lorde, A BURST OF LIGHT
Ixia Press Mineola, NY, ©1988

STORYlab12

INTEGRATION

Turning knowledge into wisdom

"One does not question miracles, or complain that they are not constructed perfectly to one's liking."

Cassandra Clare, Clockwork Princess

"My life wasn't how I planned it would be. It wasn't even close. It was a thousand times better."

Nicole Williams, Crush

"Grief is in two parts. The first is loss. The second is the remaking of life."

Anne Roiphe, Epilogue: A Memoir

"When you're on a journey and the end keeps getting further and further away, then you realize the real end is the journey."

Karlfried Graf Durckheim

"Religion is a defense against the experience of God."

Carl Jung

"The epilogue is the last word"

Laura Lentz — STORYquest

INTEGRATION

Epilogue – Master of the Two Worlds

Definition of Epilogue: a short postscript to any literary work, such as a brief description of the fates of the characters in a novel.

The epilogue is the part of your book where the Hero takes a look back over their shoulder — it's the conclusion of your book, and contains the last taste you will leave in the mouth of your reader. Think about the flavors of your book. Which one do you want to linger on the reader's tongue when the cover is finally closed? What do you want to say as you look back on your Quest — a final thought to impart to the reader now that the journey is complete.

It may not be titled "Epilogue", and not every book has one. Just like other stages of the Quest, this may not apply to your story. Think of this as your final chance to say something of importance to your reader. In *You Are Not Alone*, Debbie looks one final time back over her shoulder in chapter 18, titled *Still Transforming* — with a memory of dancing with her husband to the song "Harvest Moon," two weeks before he died. Then she offers us her final piece of wisdom and insight as she turns herself back around toward her future, her eyes upward, taking in the whole universe and inviting us to do the same.

In the *Beggar King and the Secret of Happiness*, Joel ben Izzy's Epilogue is subtitled "The Beggar King", and he finishes an epic tale of King Solomon he began in the beginning of the book. It's also a transformative ending, showing us how King Solomon, much like Joel, now has a wisdom that he had not known before — a wisdom of the heart.

In *The Color of Water*, James McBride lovingly invites his mother to his best friend's Jewish wedding, where we are able to witness her - one last time - look back over her shoulder at her Jewish past, then walk away from it one final time.

In *The Chronology of Water*, Lidia Yuknavitch's Epilogue is titled "Wisdom is a Motherfucker." Her opening sentence is "You didn't actually think I was going to leave you inside marriage and family in the regular way, did you?" She gives us final wisdom about family and how to craft our stories. The book is worth purchasing just for her epilogue. Lidia is a rogue writer — she breaks many traditional formats, which is what makes her book so riveting. Her story gives us permission to break form.

Reasons for an Epilogue:

- Often authors want to show what will happen to characters after the story's conclusion, and readers want to know this.

- An epilogue can be used to shock the reader and flip an ending on its head, such as the stunning epilogue of The Handmaid's Tale.

- An epilogue can be used to create discussion among the readers.

- An epilogue can be used to set up the next book.

- An epilogue is a reflection, a final wisdom to impart to readers.

- Characters take one final look over their shoulder and see the past from a new vantage point.

- Epilogues should be concise, not more than a page or two.

- Epilogues can pull us far into the future, when we still feel the impact of the Hero who may be long gone.

INTEGRATION

LITERARY examples

Prospero
William Shakespeare, The Tempest, Act Five, Epilogue

Now my spells are all broken,
And the only power I have is my own,
Which is very weak. Now you all
Have got the power to keep me prisoner here,
Or send me off to Naples. Please don't
Keep me here on this desert island
With your magic spells. Release me
So I can return to my dukedom
With your help. The gentle wind
You blow with your applause
Will fill my ship's sails. Without applause,
My plan to please you has failed.
Now I have no spirits to enslave,
No magic to cast spells,
And I'll end up in despair
Unless I'm relieved by prayer,
Which wins over God himself
And absolves all sins.
Just as you'd like to have your sins forgiven,
Indulge me, forgive me, and set me free.

Invictus
William Ernest Henley

Out of the night that covers me,
    Black as the pit from pole to pole,
I thank whatever gods may be
    For my unconquerable soul.

In the fell clutch of circumstance
    I have not winced nor cried aloud.
Under the bludgeonings of chance
    My head is bloody, but unbowed.

Beyond this place of wrath and tears
    Looms but the Horror of the shade,
And yet the menace of the years
    Finds and shall find me unafraid.

It matters not how strait the gate,
    How charged with punishments the scroll,
I am the master of my fate,
    I am the captain of my soul.

STORYlab12

READ

The Chronology of Water

Lidia Yuknavitch

Page 295, Wisdom is a Motherfucker

You Are Not Alone

Debbie Augenthaler

Chapter 18
Still Transforming

The Beggar King and the Secret of Happiness

Joel ben Izzy

Page 213, Epilogue
—The Beggar King

The Color of Water

James McBride

Page 279, Epilogue

INTEGRATION

createYOURstory

Writing Warm-Ups

Two-minute warm-ups prepare you for the longer writing exercises.

Set a timer for one-minute.

Use the first sentence as a starter sentence, then write for another minute using the second sentence.

Repeat.

WRITING WARM-UP 1

Indulge me, forgive me, set me free.
[write for one minute]

The only power I had was my own.
[write for another minute]

WRITING WARM-UP 2

Ten years later.
[write for one minute]

And after that.
[write for another minute]

Pre-Writing Inspiration
Sentence Wall

BEFORE YOU WRITE

Choose a sentence from this sentence wall to use as a starter sentence, or somewhere in your chapter.

When all is done, when comes that day.

Under the stars, under the sky and night.

We found beneath the larger cause our own.

Something will remain of vision and the quest.

We fought, as one by one.

No one's allowed to know his fate.

Now I can just speak the smallest word.

Lying back under the tallest, oldest trees.

My life is circled by the shadow of love.

And a mirror gives the moon back to the moon.

Which came first, memory or words?

STORYlab12

Create Your Story
Writing Instructions:

Choose the writing prompt that inspires you. Later, you can explore each prompt.

Write for thirteen minutes without stopping, or overthinking your content. Set your timer!

---

1 ONE FINAL WISDOM

*Write about something you want to tell your reader about your story
—one final wisdom to share.*
[write for 13 minutes]

2 ALL YOUR TRUTHS

Write about all your truths, a recap of truths.
[write for 13 minutes]

3 HOW THINGS TURNED OUT DIFFERENTLY

*Write something about yourself you thought you knew for sure.
Now show us how you were all wrong about your own perception of yourself
—write about how things turned out differently.*
[write for 13 minutes]

INTEGRATION

Create Your Story

Writing Instructions:

Choose the writing prompt that inspires you. Later, you can explore each prompt.

Write for thirteen minutes without stopping, or overthinking your content. Set your timer!

1 Far Back or Fast Forward

Write an epilogue that goes far back in time, before the main character is born. Or write an epilogue that fast-forwards us so far into the future that your main character is no longer alive.
[write for 13 minutes]

2 A Story You Were Told Your Whole Life

Tell us a story you were told your whole life and how you interpret it differently now.
[write for 13 minutes]

3 Something You Learned

Write about something you learned while writing your stories.
[write for 13 minutes]

STORYquest

STORYquest Resources

Books About The Hero's Journey:

The Writer's Journey, Mythic Structure for Writers by Christopher Vogler

The Hero with a Thousand Faces by Joseph Campbell

The Hero's Journey: Joseph Campbell on His Life and Work (The Collected Works of Joseph Campbell) by Joseph Campbell

Your Mythic Journey, Finding Meaning in Your Life Through Writing & Storytelling
by Sam Keen

Books by Authors of Journey Poems:

Ellen Bass:
- *Like a Beggar*
- *Mules of Love*
- *The Human Line*
- *Indigo*

Kamand Kojouri
- *The Eternal Dance*

Sharon Olds
- *Stag's Leap*

C. Dale Young
- *The Halo*

Lyn Holley Doucet
- *Reflections of the Heart, Writings from Sacred Center*

Wendi Romero
- *Pilgrimage to Self*
- *Out of the Kiln*
- *Clear a Path*

Books by Authors of Journey Poems: (continued)

Thomas R. Smith
> *Walking Before Dawn*

Constance Frenzen
> *The Voice of Poetry*
> Constance Frenzen has created *The Voice of Poetry*, a video-based website designed to increase appreciation of poetry as an art form. TheVoiceofPoetry.com

Writing Books to Inspire:

Writing From the Heart — Tapping the Power of Your Inner Voice by Nancy Aronie

Big Magic by Elizabeth Gilbert

Poemcrazy, Freeing Your Life with Words by Susan Goldsmith Woolridge

The Story Within, New Insights and Inspiration for Writers by Laura Oliver

The WAR of ART, Break Through the Blocks and Win Your Inner Creative Battles by Steven Pressfield

Sacred Stories, A Celebration of the Power of Stories to Transform and Heal by Charles Simpkinson & Anne Simpkinson

Writing Books on Craft:

"The Making of a Story" A Norton Guide to Creative Writing by Alice LaPlante

Shut Up and Write by Judy Bridges

The Art of Memoir by Mary Karr

Online Workshops

Laura Lentz & Faculty —Write with Your Peers

LITerati.academy — Laura Lentz, author and essayist, teaches 6-week intensive themed writing workshops online with writers from all over the world who want to practice craft weekly, create new material and write with their peers. Join a vibrant, active community of writers, authors, poets and guest teachers. Writers practice in intimate, small live groups to create new material and open their creative channels.

Weekly classes also meet live on the north shore of Kaua'i. Out of town writers welcome to come for extended writing sessions. Students are authors, produce podcasts and contribute to anthologies. Beginners welcome.

Writing Retreats on Kaua'i

Six-week themed writing intensives available to long term visiting writers and Kaua'i residents with author Laura Lentz. Weekend workshops and week-long intensives also available at *LITerati.academy*.

Write with Ellen Bass

Ellen has been teaching and inspiring writers for fifty years! She offers retreats and online workshops for poets and prose writers, as well as Living Room Craft Talks in which she teaches aspects of the craft of poetry. You can find out more at her website: *ellenbass.com*.

Join Our Writing Community

Find us on Facebook through STORY*quest*, the Writer, the Hero, the Journey.
Join our writing community and share your stories.

Gratitude

I could not have written this book without my students, who by their presence and passion for writing helped me shape the content. Thank you Genoa Bliven for walking into my living room on Kaua'i and then for leaving our beloved island; for suggesting I work with writers online. For students all over the world who show up every week as explorers, who have kept me in my own place of learning and discovery. You have all made me a better teacher and writer. Your hunger for diving into story has kept me creating courses and curriculum that offer the best of other poets and authors for inspiration. You remind me weekly that every literary rule is made to be shattered into something beautiful.

A big Hawaiian *mahalo* to author Debbie Augenthaler, who taught me all stories have elements of grief inside them, and who launched with me the writing workshop *Write Your Grief Story* based on the elements of the Hero's Journey. It's been a rewarding friendship, business partnership and growth experience.

To Nancy Aronie, my first writing teacher and author of *Writing From the Heart* — for crossing the swollen, stormy, fast moving Hanalei river in a small canoe with her husband Joel to show up water soaked and exuberant to teach my Kaua'i writers.

To so many inspiriting poets who loaned us their work to inspire us to write our own stories. A big hug to Ellen Bass — my friend, mentor and astonishing poet, who first made me look at my writing in a serious way.

To Larry Feinstein, for the calls at 7 a.m. to go over writing exercises, his loving direction and belief that everything I touch will turn to some kind of magic — thank you for your constant vote of confidence and for being the greatest friend and confidant an author and teacher can have. Thank you for loving and accepting all of me.

A special acknowledgement to Limor Farber — for the many long night walks, all the cooking in between chapters of this book. You are a true soul sister, friend, artist extraordinaire, book designer, poet and cheerleader — for the many conversations and brainstorms and her belief in all artists.

To "Mama Kaua'i" — for without her fire, her water, her Hanalei, the breath of the trade winds, the lightening, the storms, the swollen rivers, the raging surf and her many initiations, I would not be wild enough to continue this quest. I will never pretend to know her.

To my family — my beloved daughter Kele for arriving into my arms so we could each start our own Journey together. To her partner Kai, to my doppelgänger Mika, who reminds me every day of the magic we are all here to witness, and that time is not linear. Thank you for your heart, sharing the moon and for continuing to show me the world through your eyes. And to Connor Atlas Campbell, who came in to show us the capacity to love is endless. May you teach us all to live up to our names.

Thank you Mike Murray, a beautiful poet and art appreciator, who has witnessed the worst and best of me through co-parenting, for coming together with me to bring so many of those I love into being.

Liz Becker. You have been my spiritual compass and dear friend, a stunning writer and my greatest supporter for what feels like lifetimes. You are an official member of my family.

Thank you Mimsy, a magical storyteller and staunch supporter of seeing this class turn into a workbook for other writers.

To all my friends and family who continue to shape the human I am becoming. You know who you are.

To Philip Brautigam who designed and illustrated this book, and all the supporting materials to bring this product to life and into your hands. For his patience when this book was spread all over the floor of his studio, my hands reshaping the content, page by page. Thank you for your humor, perspective, persistence and perseverance.

Mostly I am grateful for you,— who is nurturing a story inside you, getting ready to release it to the page to teach all of us. I honor the writer in you, the teacher in you and the magic swirling around you.

May you navigate your way through life to bring your wisdom to the page.

Index – Poetry & Inspiration

After the Disaster, 127
Annunciation, 143
Any Common Desolation, 104
Archaic Torso of Apollo, 24
Augenthaler, Debbie, xvii

Bass, Ellen, 104, 136, 146
Beck, Virginia, 88
Broken Wing, 66

Carnal Knowledge, 152
Cavafy, C. P., xv
Che, Cathy Linh, 113

Darkest Night, My, 105
Deutsch, Abigail, 127

Fertile Ground, 9
Frenzen, Constance, 152

Grief & The Hero's Journey, xvii

Henley, William Ernest, 181

I Was an Earth Angel, 55
Initiation, The, 74
Instructions for the Journey, 72
Invictus, 181
Ithaka, xv

Lentz, Laura, 39, 55, 72, 74, 105, 166

Magician, The, 166
My Mother Upon Hearing News of Her Mother's Death, 113

Ordinary Boy, An, 8
Out of the Silence, 88

Prospero, 180

Refusal, My, 39
Relax, 136
Rilke, Rainer Maria, 24
Romero, Wendi, 9, 66

Shakespeare, William, 180
Smith, Thomas R., 95
Sterner, Cheryl, 138

The Thing Is, 146
Trust, 95
Young, C. Dale, 8, 143